A Bibliography of Business Ethics, 1971-1975

Publications of the Colgate Darden Graduate School of Business Administration of the University of Virginia

Bank Expansion in Virginia, 1962–1966: The Holding Company and the Direct Merger. By Paul Foster.

Basic Research in Finance: Needs and Prospects. By Charles C. Abbott.

A Financial Planning Model for Private Colleges: A Research Report. By William J. Arthur.

Forty Years of Public Utility Finance. By Harold H. Young.

Management of Small Enterprises: Cases and Readings. Edited by William Rotch.

A Selected Bibliography of Applied Ethics in the Professions, 1950–1970. By Daniel L. Gothie.

Stettinius, Sr.: Portrait of a Morgan Partner. By John D. Forbes.

Business Ethics and Social Responsibilities: Theory and Practice. Conference Proceedings. Edited by Daniel L. Gothie.

Report on the Teaching of Socio-Ethical Issues in Collegiate Schools of Business/Public Administration. Edited by Thomas F. McMahon.

The Pension Return Law of 1974: Impact on American Society. Conference Proceedings. Edited by Paul M. Hammaker.

The First Twenty Years: The Darden School at Virginia. Edited by C. Stewart Sheppard.

A Bibliography of Business Ethics, 1971-1975

DONALD G. JONES

University Press of Virginia
Charlottesville

The publication of this study has been assisted by the Center for the Study of Applied Ethics, Graduate School of Business Administration, University of Virginia

THE UNIVERSITY PRESS OF VIRGINIA

First published 1977

Library of Congress Cataloging in Publication Data

Jones, Donald G
    A bibliography of business ethics, 1971–1975.

    A continuation of the bibliography by D. L. Gothie published in 1973.
    Sponsored by the Center for the Study of Applied Ethics, Colgate Darden Graduate School of Business Administration, University of Virginia.
    1. Business ethics—Bibliography. I. Gothie, Daniel L. A selected bibliography of applied ethics in the professions, 1950–1970. II. Colgate Darden Graduate School of Business Administration. Center for the Study of Applied Ethics. III. Title.
Z7164.C81J59 [HF5387]   016.174   76–52486

ISBN 0–8139–0711–X

Printed in the United States of America

Foreword

It has been three years since the Center for the Study of Applied Ethics at the Darden Graduate Business School presented its first bibliography on significant publications in the area of applied ethics. During these years, public interest in and concern with ethical considerations have generated such a spate of literature that a second edition of the bibliography appears to be desirable. The extensive writings on ethics, however, have compelled us to restrict coverage to those we regard as important to the world of business. The size of this volume is evidence that even with this restriction the task has been a formidable one.

We have been most fortunate in being able to attract Professor Donald Jones to serve as a Research Associate of the Center during his sabbatical leave from Drew University. His introduction to the bibliography reveals a penetrating insight into the "state of the art" based on impressive academic and practical experience.

It is our hope that this bibliography will serve the needs of many different kinds of libraries, but more importantly its main purpose will have been met if individuals take the cited works from the shelves and settle down to careful study.

The Center for the Study of Applied Ethics seeks to ameliorate the dissatisfaction, if not downright antipathy, toward business in our society. Through research, publications, conferences, and cooperation with similarly oriented organizations, the Center is building on the assumption that it is possible for business to attain and maintain high levels of ethical standards and practices. In order to justify this assumption, consistent attention and study must be given to ethical issues, and this bibliography offers a valuable resource in the charting of such a course of serious inquiry.

C. STEWART SHEPPARD
Dean of The Colgate Darden Graduate
School of Business Administration
University of Virginia

Acknowledgments

My gratitude goes immediately to Dean C. Stewart Sheppard for his cooperative support and encouragement and the wise counsel he gave in his winsome fashion throughout this project. My thanks also go to Henry Wingate of the Darden School Library and his staff for the expert assistance given in the final stages of manuscript preparation.

Finally my thanks go out to two industrious and intelligent research assistants from Drew University. Susan Akers and Joy Harrington shared in virtually every stage of preparation of this bibliography, spending long hours in various libraries not only gathering data but making significant editorial contributions. For their devotion to the task, sense of humor, and special qualities of creativity I am extremely grateful.

DONALD G. JONES

Madison, New Jersey
November 1976

Contents

Introduction

Background and Focus of the Book

This volume is a bibliographic reference guide on business ethics covering the five-year span 1971 through 1975. It is composed primarily of materials in English published in the United States and has been selectively annotated. The items cited here cover the full range of subject matter in business ethics along a continuum from the pole of personal integrity and the private ethics of executives to the wider, complex institutional issues of business and society relations.

Completed under the aegis of the Center for the Study of Applied Ethics, this book fulfills a commitment to update at intervals of five years a bibliography on applied ethics and the professions. As it turns out, there is some deviation from the original intention. The first volume covering the years 1950 through 1970 included materials on government and politics, the health sciences, law, physical and life sciences, and social sciences.[1] The present bibliography is narrower in scope, including only those books, essays, articles, and monographs that properly come under the rubric "business ethics."

The decision to focus on socioethical issues and business at the exclusion of other professions was based on two factors. The first and more important has to do with the recent proliferation of written materials on professional ethics in general and business ethics in particular. The sheer quantity of entries in a comprehensive bibliography would have made it an impractical project. A second factor in forming the decision is the appearance over the past few years of other bibliographic publications dealing with professional and social ethics, precluding the necessity of an inclusive bibliography of applied ethics and the professions.

1. Gothie, Daniel L., *A Selected Bibliography of Applied Ethics in the Professions, 1950-1970* (Charlottesville, Virginia: University Press of Virginia, 1973).

The outline of the bibliography with the various subheadings as set forth in the table of contents is for the most part self-evident as to its significance and meaning, but a few interpretive comments are in order.

Following the first section, "Business Ethics—General Works," are the two major sections comprising the bulk of the book. The first, "Business Ethics and the Functional Areas of Management," may be termed the *microethics* section. The second, "Business and Social Responsibility," may be called *macroethics*. These categories in fact represent the two basic aspects and approaches to business ethics. I want to avoid the error of simply identifying business ethics with either the narrower ethical issues that arise out of the day-to-day decision-making in the functional areas of management or the broader socioethical issues that emerge out of the intersection of corporate activity with the various publics in society.

There are those who would put the broad area of "Business and Social Responsibility" (sometimes labeled "Business and Society") alongside, but keep it distinct from, business ethics. This view rests on a misunderstanding of ethics and the scope of ethical discourse. To be acquainted with the literature that falls under the heading "Business and Social Responsibility" is to be aware of the constant use of such terms as "corporate obligation," "public good," "social benefit," "corporate social performance," "solving society's problems," and "legitimacy and the credibility crisis." Such language is a clear signal to students of ethics that whatever else is going on in terms of sociological description, business reasoning, and economic analysis, the authors are engaged in ethical discourse.

Pervading all of this literature are implicit, if not explicit, assumptions as to what is "good" for persons in the business community and those affected by business behavior. Normative judgments articulating the range between permissible and nonpermissible corporate behavior with a view to minimizing social and personal injury abound. Even the arguments opposing the social responsibility doctrine by such figures as F. A. Hayek and Milton Friedman do not proceed without some appeals to maximizing wider human benefit, which, incidentally, is in continuity with the tradition of Adam Smith, that great moral philosopher of the eighteenth century. In sum, all of the materials included under the category "Business and Social Responsibility" pass the minimal tests of what constitutes ethical discourse. The burden of defining more precisely the meaning of ethics will be assumed below.

The final two sections of the bibliography are highly selective and limited in scope. Books and articles under the heading "Theoretical and Applied Ethics" address issues of pure ethical theory, the application of ethics to social and economic issues, and in particular the question of justice and the economic order. The list of entries is simply illustrative of the area of philosophical and religious ethics and representative of the different kinds of scholarly works available in the field of ethics. Notwithstanding the numerical and substantive limitations of this section, it is hoped that readers will be pointed to resources that will enhance conceptual clarity and deepen the intellectual grasp of business ethics.

The last section, "Religion and Business Ethics," is hardly inclusive of all the statements, pronouncements, and editorials that have issued forth from the churches and religious journals in the past few years; but an attempt has been made to make the entries representative. A perusal of the literature in this section reveals two interesting things. There has been a head-on clash between some Protestant social activists and big business in the past five years, especially in the area of investment policy and social justice; and in fact, that confrontation has resulted in changes in corporate behavior. But the more important point that can be made as a result of gathering these data is to note the sheer paucity of significant scholarly work to come out of the institutional church or the theological enterprise. With few exceptions little in the way of rigorous analytical materials or intellectually penetrating prophetic writings have been produced by the professional clergy, theologians, and religious ethicists on the subject of business ethics in the past few years.

Certainly the clerics and professional ethicists had much more to say in the early sixties after revelations of such misdeeds as the electric companies' price-fixing scandals, the Billy Sol Estes affair, payolla in the record industry, corruption in television game shows, and the Great Salad Oil Scandal. Indeed, there were a number of very good studies produced then by Roman Catholic and Protestant scholars that still comprise a significant body of relevant literature on business ethics.

During the past five years, for some reason, the moralists in the religious community have been much more interested in addressing issues in biomedical ethics than in business ethics. Jewish and Christian social ethicists are involved in all of the existing institutes and centers of biomedical ethics and have played leading roles in the numerous symposia and workshop activities covering that area. There has been no comparable involvement in business ethics. Why? What reasons are there for this apparent lack of attention to the religious quarter to socioethical issues in business? What is the status of business and religion and their various interrelations in American society? The very brevity of this last section in the bibliography invites such queries and raises cultural issues of sociological importance.

Purpose and Significance of the Bibliography

The purposes of this bibliography are multiple. In the first instance it continues the development of a working data base for the Center for the Study of Applied Ethics at the Colgate Darden Graduate School of Business Administration, University of Virginia. Its larger purpose is to provide a reference tool and information resource for scholars, business managers, and other interested parties. In fulfilling this primary function, the bibliography should be of special value to consultants and business managers who are involved in the formation of new ethical guidelines, codes of conduct, and policies that relate to socioethical matters. It should also serve the academic researcher well. But it is my hope that the contribution of this volume goes beyond its primary value as a research tool.

For instance, aspects of this bibliography may have some sociological significance as noted above in the comments on the paucity of religious authorship. Related to that and no less interesting, in a sociological sense, is the fact that most of the discussion about business ethics over the past five years has been carried on by professional business managers and teachers in business schools. We might have expected that certified reformers, do-gooders, and perennial critics of business would be in the vanguard. The ironical fact of the matter, however, is that the American business community—not usually given to moralizing—has provided the largest portion of the authorship cited here. And the vast majority of the articles cited are from business journals.

What does this mean? In a comparative sense it could mean that the business community, more than any other professional group, is taking the initiative in coming to grips with the ethical crisis of our society. Whether or not this is the case, the very quantity and variety of entries in this bibliography covering just five years would seem to indicate important changes occurring in the business world. While it is still true that business managers and teachers are pragmatic and tend to be positivistic and technologically oriented, it is also the case that perhaps more than at any other time in the history of modern business there is an awareness of the ethical dimensions of decision-making and policy formation. The literature here stands as clear testimony to the fact that self-criticism, internal pressures to raise standards of conduct, and increased sensitivity to social responsibilities are becoming part of the changing business ethos. Aside from the witness of the sheer size of the bibliography, the subsection on "Changing Society and Business: New Realities" includes numerous entries to support such a conclusion.

In commenting on the purposes and significance of this bibliography, it should also be noted that such a publication has symbolic value. The whole has special symbolic value and meaning beyond the sum of its parts inasmuch as it mirrors and participates in critical moments and trends of the past half decade. The burgeoning literature in business ethics represented here may be viewed as a type of response to the most dramatic story of the period, Watergate. It also reflects in crisp outline such sociohistorical currents as the new consumerism, the struggle for minority justice, the ecological crisis, the impact of the multinationals, and stricter demands for occupational health and safety. The volume as a whole would also seem to stand as a mirror and symbol of what some have called an "ethical crisis" in our public life or, at least, the raised consciousness about ethical issues in business and society relations.

Finally, I would hope that this bibliography would make a contribution in shaping and defining the subject of business ethics. As I gathered and gave form to the contents it became obvious at the outset that such a task was much more than a clerk's job. Because the field itself is not well defined, certain initiatives had to be taken and judgments made without clear antecedent guidelines. Such necessary risks are the means of advancing scholarship.

To establish broad categories and subtypes of ethical issues and problem areas is to provide a mode not only for organizing reference data but for understanding and structuring the discipline itself. I remember well when the first comprehensive bio-medical ethics bibliographies came out a few years ago how the very divisions into ethical problem areas served to define the discipline, affect classroom course development, and clarify research areas. It is intended that the appearance of this volume taken together with former bibliographies may have a similar pedagogical function.

In a very practical sense I would hope that the structure and divisions might have a pedagogical effect in helping individual instructors, administrators, and personnel development managers to set up courses and seminars and to formulate curricula in which ethics plays a part. In a more general and indirect sense a contribution may be made in the direction of defining what is now a confusing area. Even a debate engendered by this book may serve to that end. For instance, I would expect that many readers would want to quibble about nomenclature and disagree about the understanding of the subject matter and the way it has been sliced. Such critical discussion, it is hoped, would enhance our common grasp of what business ethics is and help to shape it as a coherent and solid discipline.

What Is Ethics?

Informing the development of this bibliography is an understanding of ethics which should now be briefly articulated[2]. In the basic sense of the term *ethics is the practical and rational enterprise of reflecting on the right and good of human life*. Ethics deals with the "what should be done?" questions with reference to actions that might harm or benefit human beings. Ethics proceeds from the vantage point of certain values, principles, and rules in proscribing actions that would cause personal or social injury, deny human rights, or violate basic human dignity and in prescribing conduct that aims at minimizing human harm and maximizing human benefit.

Insofar as most corporate policies and executive decisions do affect the welfare of people directly or indirectly, it can be sharply noted that ethics is an inextricable part of business activity. In other words, a manager who makes a business decision without the aid of ethical reflection is being denied full access to information and dimensions of the problem at hand. By providing models of decision-making and criteria by which actions are judged, ethics widens the information base, thus enhancing the capacity to predict long-range costs and benefits.

Ethics, of course, does not always provide certain guidance. Frequently people of sound reason and goodwill will differ as to what is right or wrong. It should also be clearly affirmed that ethics alone is impotent and irrelevant. Ethical reflection alone does not provide clear guidelines on such matters as fair hiring practices, truth in advertising, proper foreign payments, and the limits of business social responsibility. In treating these and similar issues responsible ethical reflection would join business reasoning and economic analysis. Moreover, ethical principles, to be relevant, must go to school with nonethical facts. One prominent ethicist put it pungently: "Ethics aren't worth a damn without facts." In fact, ethical perplexity in bus-

2. For a much more sophisticated definition, see the essay "Basic Terms in the Study of Religious Ethics" by David Little and Sumner Twiss, Jr., in Gene Outka and John P. Reeder, *Religion and Morality* (New York: Harper and Row, 1973).

iness is often reduced greatly if not dissolved completely by the proper assessment of relevant factual matters. Noting the limitations of ethics in and of itself should not obscure its importance in improving conceptual clarity about business issues and, in particular, sharpening our vision as to the moral meaning of business actions.

Four Features of Ethics

The above understanding of ethics can be further elaborated and specified by pointing to four basic features in the definition of ethics.

1. The first and most important feature is the *other-regarding point of view*. For a decision, action, or policy to pass the test of ethics it has to be shown that due consideration for all persons or social agencies affected has been given. The ethical point of view as other-regardingness is the view that considers the legitimate interests and moral claims of all interested parties. Further, it means seeing the effects of the action from the point of view of the interested parties. Here the application of the rule of reciprocity well known as the *golden rule* is a good test of other-regardingness. If a marketing manager were to view a pricing decision from the point of view of the shareholders or one's own gain without assessing pricing obligations to competitors, purchasers, consumers, and other interested parties, we would say that that manager did not adopt an ethical point of view.

Another dimension of the other-regarding features is the recognition of humans as ends in themselves. The well-known Kantian maxim says it well: "Treat humans as ends and not as means only." To deny persons the freedom to consent or dissent regarding actions that affect their own destiny is to violate this basic ethical requirement. For instance, whenever a purchaser, whether professional or lay, is denied adequate information or given misinformation about a product, we would call that unethical because it violates the other-regarding feature inasmuch as the freedom to consent or dissent is denied.

Another way of expressing the meaning of other-regardingness is to use the phrase "people oriented." Corporations claiming that they exist by and for people are admitting to the ethical point of view and should be so judged.

2. The second feature is *superiority*. In a context of several points of view the ethical point of view is superior to all others because ethical criteria have to do with human ends. In common language we use terms such as "unfair," "you broke your promise," "that was dishonest," "it is unsafe," "that is inconsistent"—these and similar terms express a certain weightiness about what is at stake in a particular

action. They touch such issues as fundamental rights, duties, and specifically human ends. Hence, one can take seriously the point of view of a political party, senior management, or one's own family, but when asking the question "what should I do?" when facing a straight of conscience and competing points of view, ethical action guides will claim superiority. The ethical point of view is the overriding viewpoint if the matter at hand is in fact a weighty issue.

3. Ethics is a *rational* enterprise. This third feature, rationality, points to both the process of decision-making and the practical justification of an action or proposal. Clear thinking, objectivity, orderly procedure, and systematic analysis are intrinsic to the ethical enterprise. To be an ethical professional person is then to assume the burden of rational decision-making and rational defense of positions taken. We may use the commonplace phrase, "let conscience be your guide," if by conscience we mean what the scholastic and Puritan moralists meant, "the rule of right reason." On the other hand, if conscience means some private and subjective nonrational monitor on conduct, the word is highly misleading and should be banished from usage as too sentimental and totally irrelevant to the complexities of large organizations and the interdependencies of our institutional life. To be ethical in contemporary corporate life requires much more than personal integrity and a sense of high values. It is to be able to carefully apply well-tested ethical action guides to a real world that has been carefully examined and to be prepared to give reasons for what is being recommended. In other words, a business manager contemplating "whistle-blowing" as a response to an ethical dilemma would be well advised to think carefully about such an action and to be prepared to proffer good reasons for such an action or inaction as a better part of prudence and as an ethical requirement.

4. Ethics is a *practical* enterprise. This is a feature of ethics about which all ethicists are agreed. From Aristotle through Augustine, Kant, and Niebuhr, ethics has been viewed as an activity, an enterprise, a system, or a way of thinking that aims to guide and influence action. In contrast to theoretical modes of inquiry, practical reasoning offers guidance for such existential questions as "what should I do?" or "how can I do the right thing?"

As a practical enterprise, the task of ethics is fourfold:

a. to help settle moral disputes when there is a genuine conflict between licit claims of interest and/or competing ethical values;

b. to offer practical justification for actions done or proposed;

c. to recommend policies, actions, or codes; and,

d. to evaluate actions and policies.

The goal of ethical reflection then, in whatever form, is practical knowledge.

Business Ethics as Social Ethics

Business ethics is a subdiscipline of the larger field of ethics and properly comes under the special area known as social ethics. As such, business is another instance in which a sphere of life—in this case the commercial sphere—is viewed from the perspective of ethics, and is an activity analogous to political ethics, medical ethics, ecological ethics, ethics of marriage and family, ethics and race relations, sexual ethics, and the ethics of various other spheres of life.

As a subdiscipline of social ethics, business ethics is primarily concerned with institutional arrangements, policies, corporate politics, and the social ethos of business decision-making and action. However important individual behavior and personal integrity are, business ethics should not be confused with personal morality. As Reinhold Niebuhr has taught, "a sharp distinction must be drawn between the moral and social behavior of individuals and social groups." The assumption underlying this distinction is that not only is the context of decision-making quite different when an individual is in a one-to-one relationship in the living room and when he or she is implementing corporate goals in a complex organization, but that the ethical requirements of institutional and private life are frequently different. Certainly any analysis of permissible or nonpermissible behavior in big business is at best shallow if viewed only from the perspective of individual morality. The current bribery issue is a good case in point. To treat the matter of questionable foreign payments by business firms in terms of the personal integrity of some business managers is to miss the complexities of the issue and to render any judgments about the right or wrong of such actions meaningless. As a current topic of business ethics, the issue of bribery and unusual foreign payments must be seen in light of company policies, unwritten expectations, financial pressures, and traditions and customs of foreign countries and against the background of the changing market mechanism of international business. Only then can there be a meaningful ethical judgment on what is a justifiable or nonjustifiable payment.

Business ethics goes beyond individual morality also in the sense in which it attends to broader societal issues as they intersect with normal business goals and techniques. These broad and complex socio-ethical issues are becoming more and more integral to managerial decision-making, hence the current relevance of ethics. As much of the literature advises, professional managers need to engage in ethical reflection to be equipped to factor into their decision-making such tangibles as national interest, energy conservation, public health and safety, fair competition, community betterment, minority justice, and air, earth, and water quality. To do this is to be involved in the application of ethics to business. So understood, business ethics is not just a current fad; rather, it is becoming a long-term condition of fact.

Business Ethics: General Works

Business Ethics: General Works

Books

Acton, Harry Burrows. *The Ethics of Capitalism*. London: Foundation for Business Responsibilities, 1972.

Acton, Harry Burrows. *The Morals of Markets: An Ethical Exploration*. London: Harlow Longman, 1971.
A philosophical and ethical vindication of free enterprise.

Adolph, Peter. *Atlantic Acceptance Scandal*. New York: Stein and Day, 1973.

Backman, Jules, ed. *Business Problems of the Seventies*. New York: New York University Press, 1973.
Includes discussion of business obligations.

Barnet, Richard J. *The Crisis of the Corporation*. New York: AMA-COM, American Management Associations, 1975.
The crisis of the corporation is at heart a crisis of belief. Society doesn't trust business to act ethically.

Benham, Thomas W. *Trends in Public Attitudes Towards Business and the Free Enterprise System*. Washington, D.C.: White House Conference on the Industrial World Ahead, February 1972.
The president of Opinion Research Corporation presents current findings.

Brozen, Yale. *Competitive Economy*, Vol. I. Morristown, New Jersey: General Learning Press, 1975.

Bump, Glen H. *How to Succeed in Business Without Being a Pagan*. Wheaton, Illinois: Scripture Press, 1974.

Christian, Portia and Richard Hicks, eds. *Ethics in Business Conduct: Selected References from the Record, Problems, Attempted Solutions, Place in Business Education*. (Management Information Guides Series No. 21). Detroit: Gale, 1970. (Distributed 1971).

This is an annotated bibliography on business ethics covering the years 1960–1970.

Clapp, Jane. *Professional Ethics and Insignia.* Metuchen, New Jersey: Scarecrow Press, 1974.

Cohen, Peter. *The Gospel According to the Harvard Business School.* Garden City, New York: Doubleday & Co., 1973.
A muckraking exposé by a former MBA candidate at the Harvard Business School.

Cohn, Jules. *The Conscience of the Corporation: Business and Urban Affairs 1967–1970.* Baltimore: The Johns Hopkins Press, 1971.

Coleman, Bruce P. and John W. Bonge. *Concepts for Corporate Strategy: Readings in Business Policy.* New York: Macmillan, 1972.
The volume attends to business socio-ethical issues.

Directory of Corporate Social Policy Courses in Graduate Business Schools and Professors Who Teach Them. Chicago, Illinois: National Affiliation of Concerned Business students, October 1, 1974.

Dowd, Douglas F. *The Twisted Dream: Capitalist Development in the U.S. Since 1776.* Cambridge, Mass: Winthrop Pub., 1973.

Drucker, Peter F. *Management: Tasks, Responsibilities, Practices.* New York: Harper and Row, 1974.

Flory, Charles D. and R. Alec Mackenzie. *The Credibility Gap in Management.* New York: Van Nostrand Reinhold, 1971.

Fuller, John Grant. *200,000,000 Guinea Pigs.* New York: Putnam, 1972.
An exposé of new dangers in everyday foods, drugs, cosmetics.

Goldston, Eli and others. *The American Business Corporation: New Perspectives on Profit and Purpose.* Cambridge, Massachusetts: M. I. T. Press, 1972.

Gothie, Daniel L. *Business Ethics and Social Responsibilities: Theory and Practice.* Charlottesville, Virginia: University of Virginia, the Colgate Darden Graduate School of Business Administration, Center for the Study of Applied Ethics, 1974.
Proceedings of a conference with articles by George Steiner, Kirk O. Hansen, David Collier, Bruce Henderson and Thomas McMahon.

4

Gothie, Daniel L. *A Selected Bibliography of Applied Ethics in the Professions, 1950–1970.* Charlottesville, Virginia: University Press of Virginia, 1973.

Green, Mark J. *The Monopoly Makers: The Report on Regulations and Competition.* New York: Grossman, 1973.

Green, Mark J., Beverly C. Moore, Jr. and Bruce Wasserstein. *The Closed Enterprise System.* New York: Grossman, 1972.

Haas, John J. *Beyond Management.* Brooklyn: Theodore Gaus' Sons, Inc., 1974.
This is a brief study of business ethics and corporate responsibility seen in the context of changing economic and social trends.

Hapgood, David. *The Screwing of the Average Man.* New York: Bantam, 1975.

Heilbroner, Robert L., et al. *In the Name of Profit: Profiles in Corporate Responsibility.* New York: Doubleday & Company, 1972.
Collection of case histories about alleged corporate crime, irresponsibility and immorality.

Hickel, Walter J. *Who Owns America?* Englewood Cliffs, New Jersey: Prentice Hall, 1971.

Jacius, Michael James, Bernard A. Deitzer and William Schneider. *Elements of Managerial Action.* Homewood, Illinois: Richard D. Irwin, 1973.
See chapter 19 "The Executive and Ethics."

Jacoby, Neil H. *Corporate Power and Responsibility.* New York: Macmillan, 1973.

Jaspan, Isaac A. *Mind Your Own Business.* Englewood Cliffs, New Jersey: Prentice Hall, 1974.
A guide to recognizing, stopping but most of all preventing corporate in-house theft and other misdeeds.

Jay, Anthony. *Corporation Man: Who He Is, What He Does, Why His Ancient Tribal Impulses Dominate the Life of the Modern Corporation.* New York: Random House, 1971.
Insights from the perspective of cultural anthropology into the ethos of the business community are given in this volume. The ethics of the firm are revealed inadvertantly.

Jennings, Eugene E. *Executive in Crisis*. New York: McGraw-Hill, 1972.

Johnson, Harold L. *Business in Contemporary Society: Framework and Issues*. Belmont, California: Wadsworth, 1971.

Kapp, William K. *The Social Costs of Private Enterprise*. New York: Schocken, 1971.
First published in 1950 this volume examines the social costs of pollution, energy depletion, impairment of human life, soil erosion, and deforestation.

Lodge, George C. *The New American Ideology: How the Ideological Basis of Legitimate Authority in America is Being Radically Transformed*. New York: Knopf, 1975.
The author notes the profound implications for corporations in the social fact that our rhetoric and ideology of individualism does not correspond to the facts of corporate life.

McMahon, Thomas F. *Report on the Teaching of Socio-Ethical Issues in Collegiate Schools of Business/Public Administration*. Charlottesville, Virginia: University of Virginia, the Colgate Darden Graduate School of Business Administration, Center for the Study of Applied Ethics, 1975.
A well documented survey with useful interpretive materials.

Mendelson, Mary Adelaide. *Tender Loving Greed*. New York, New York: Knopf, 1974.
An exposé of the nursing home industry.

Nader, Ralph ed. *Whistle Blowing: The Report of the Conference on Professional Responsibility*. ed. by Ralph Nader, Peter J. Petkas and Kate Blackwell, New York: Grossman, 1972.

Okun, Arthur M. *Equality and Efficiency: The Big Trade Off*. Washington, D.C.: The Brookings Institute, 1975.
An examination of competing values in society and business with particular emphasis on the conflict between the social benefits of efficiency and the democratic value of equality. This is a well reasoned and documented study in ethical trade off.

Packard, Vance. *The Pyramid Climbers*. Fawcett World, 1971.

Perrow, Charles. *Radical Attack on Business*. New York: Harcourt Brace Jovanovich, 1972.

6

Peters, Charles and Taylor Branch. *Blowing the Whistle: Dissent in the Public Interest.* New York: Praeger, 1972.

Preston, Lee E. *The Industry and Enterprise Structure of the U.S. Economy.* New York: General Learning Press, 1973.

Robertson, James. *Profit or People? The New Social Role of Money.* London: Calder & Boyars Ltd., 1975.
An argument for an honest, just and fair money system.

Rodman, Irwin L. *The Executive Jungle.* Paperback Library, 1973.

Schrag, Philip C. *Counsel for the Deceived.* New York: Pantheon Books, 1972.

Seifert, Harvey. *Ethical Resources for Political and Economic Decision.* Philadelphia, Pennsylvania: The Westminster Press, 1972.

Sethi, Prakash S. *Up Against the Corporate Wall: Modern Corporations and Social Issues of the Seventies.* Englewood Cliffs: Prentice Hall, 1973. (Second edition).
Case studies of business socio-ethical issues with a good bibliography.

Shenfield, Barbara. *Company Boards: Their Responsibilities to Shareholders, Employees, and the Community.* Verry, 1971. (Political and Economic Planning Series).

Tarnowieski, Dale. *The Changing Business Ethic.* New York: AMACOM, 1973.

Yankelovitch, Daniel. *The New Morality: A Profile of American Youth in the Seventies.* New York: McGraw-Hill, 1973.

Articles

"Action Program for Elimination of Unethical Practices in the Engagement of Professional Services." *Proceedings of the American Society of Civil Engineers* 101 (April 1975): 267–286.

Adam, John, Jr. "Put Profit in Its Place." *Harvard Business Review* (July-August 1973): 88–98.

"After Watergate: Putting Business Ethics in Perspective." *Business Week* (September 15, 1973): 178+.

"Are New Business Ethics Beyond Reality?" *Industry Week* 168 (January 11, 1971): 51–54.

"Associations and Ethics: Are Today's Standards High Enough?" *Association Management* 27 (April 1975): 41–44.

Bacot, Eugene. "All's Fair?" *Business Administration* (December 1970): 15–17+.

Bartolomé, Fernando. "Executives as Human Beings." *Harvard Business Review* 50 (November-December 1972): 62–69.
Discusses role conflict between on-the-job and at-home realities.

Bell, Daniel and others. "Corporations and Conscience: The Issues." *Sloan Management Review* 13 (Fall 1971): 1–24.

Bennis, Warren. "Have We Gone Overboard on the Right to Know?" *Saturday Review* (March 6, 1976): 18–21.

Berlo, David K. "Morality or Ethics? Two Approaches to Organizational Control." *The Personnel Administrator* 20 (April 1975): 16–19.
The author articulates a distinction between the terms morality and ethics and argues for a firm basis in social ethics as a means of organizational maintenance and control.

Blumberg, Phillip I. "Corporate Responsibility and the Employee's Duty of Loyalty and Obedience: A Preliminary Inquiry." *Oklahoma Law Review* (August 1971): 270–318.
A change in the hierarchy of loyalties is required.

Blumenthal, Michael W. "Business Ethics: A Call for a Moral Approach." *Financial Executive* 44 (January 1976): 32–34.

Blumenthal, Michael W. "New Business Watchdog Needed." *New York Times* (May 25, 1975).
For responses to this plan for an in-house ethics committee, see the *New York Times,* June 15, 1975.

Brudney, Victor and Marvin A. Chirelstein. "Fair Shares in Corporate Mergers and Takeovers." *Harvard Law Review* 88 (December 1974): 297–346.
Sharing formula to provide fair treatment to all parties to the merger.

Burgen, Carl. "How Companies React to the Ethics Crisis." *Business Week* (February 9, 1976): 78–79.
  A brief report on concrete corporate responses to current demands on business to behave.

"Business Executives and Moral Dilemmas: A *Business and Society Review* Survey." *Business and Society Review* 13 (Spring 1975): 51–57.
  The article includes the cases submitted to the presidents of the 500 largest companies in the U.S. and also the findings.

Carroll, Archie B. "Managerial Ethics: A Post-Watergate View." *Business Horizons* 18 (April 1975): 75–80.

Carroll, Archie B. "A Survey of Managerial Ethics: Is Business Morality Watergate Morality?" *Business and Society Review* 13 (Spring 1975): 58–60.
  Findings of a research study on how business managers perceive ethical issues in business.

Chilson, F. "Corporate Ethics and White Collar Crime." *Drug and Cosmetic Industry* 113 (November 1973): 89–90.

Cleveland, Harlan. "Systems, Purposes, and the Watergate." *Operations Research* (September/October 1973): 1019+.

Cook, Franklin H. "Guidelines: A System of Ethics for Corporations." September 1973. Speech at American Business Law Association, Knoxville, Tennessee.

"Corporations and Conscience: The Issues." *Sloan Management Review* 13 (Fall 1971): 1–24.

Cushman, Robert. "Let's Put Our House in Order: A Businessman's Plea." *Business and Society Review* 15 (Winter 1975–76): 49–52.
  The author, president of Norton Company, says it's time for business people to take a stand on ethical issues. He proposes an ethics committee to be formed by business leaders.

Dahl, Robert. "Alternate Ways of Controlling Corporate Power." Address given at the Nader Conference on Corporate Accountability, 1971.

Dahl, Robert. "A Prelude to Corporate Reform." *Business and Society Review* 1 (Spring 1972): 17–23.

Downs, Anthony and R. Joseph Monsen. "Public Goods and Private Status." *Public Interest* (Spring 1971): 64–77.

Drucker, Peter. "The Concept of the Corporation." *Business and Society Review* 3 (Autumn 1972): 12–17.
This prominent author discusses the changing ethos of business and the new notion of responsibility.

Eberstadt, Nicholas N. "What History Tells Us About Corporate Responsibility." *Business and Society Review/Innovation* 7 (Autumn 1973): 76–81.
A good brief historical sketch of business responsiveness to its host environments in terms of responsible and irresponsible behavior. The author insists that today's corporate responsibility movement is an attempt to restore a 2,000-year-old western tradition.

Epstein, Edwin M. "The Historical Enigma of Corporate Legitimacy." *California Law Review* 60 (November 1972): 1701–1717.

Etzioni, Amitai. "There Oughta Be a Law—Or Should There Be?" *Business and Society Review/Innovation* 8 (Winter 1973–74): 10–11.
higher ethical behavior.
How to enforce, implement and legitimize the law to assume

Feldman, A. and A. Kirman. "Fairness and Envy." *American Economic Review* 64 (December 1974): 995–1005.

Fulmer, R. M. "Business Ethics: Present and Future." *Personnel Administration* 34 (September 1971): 48–55.

Garrett, Ray. "Changing Concepts in Business Ethics." *Business Lawyer* 30 (March 1975): 7–12.

Goodman, Charles S. and C. Merle Crawford. "Young Executives: A Source of New Ethics?" *Personnel Journal* 53 (March 1974): 180–186.
An empirical study revealing that young business students do not express a higher ethics.

"Groups Urge Advocacy Roles for Professionals." *Chemical and Engineering News* 49 (May 24, 1971): 15–16.

Hammaker, Paul M. "Ethics and the Businessman." A presentation at the Golden Anniversary Celebration of Virginia State Chamber of Commerce, Richmond, Virginia May 9, 1974.

Hanson, Walter E. "Focus on Fraud." *Financial Executive* 43 (March 1975): 14–19.

Through a realistic focus on managerial fraud, "we can give shape to the emerging new ethic in management," declares the author.

Hill, Iuan. "Associations and Ethics: Are Today's Standards High Enough?" (Association Management). *Journal of the American Society of Association Executives* 27 (April 1975): 41–44.

Holden, G. Frederic. "Ethics in Industry—The Dilemma." *Chemical Engineering* (December 10, 1973): 130+.

Hyman, Stanley. "Conscience and the Corporation." *Management Today* (September 1970): 108–111+.

Ingram, Timothy. "On Muckrakers and Whistle Blowers." *Business and Society Review* 3 (Autumn 1972): 21–30.

"Is Professional Ethics Dead?" *Civil Engineering* 44 (November 1974): 71–73.

Jacobs, Leslie W. "Business Ethics and the Law: Obligations of a Corporate Executive." *The Business Lawyer* (July 1973): 1063+.

Jessup, John K. and Irving Kristol. "On 'Capitalism' and the Free Society." *Public Interest* (Winter 1971): 101–105.

Jones, D. C. "Levin: Equity Funding Bribed Former Illinois Department Officer." *National Underwriters* 79 (April 19, 1975): 1+.

Kandel, William. "The Social Conscience in Hard Times." *Business and Society Review/Innovation* 8 (Winter 1973–74): 17–20.

Discusses the difficulties of others regarding responsibility when the economy is down.

Keith, R. J. "Dispense with the Defensive." *Sales Management* 106 (March 15, 1971): 37–38+.

"Kemper Tells Corporate America to Ostracize Its Unethical Members." *National Underwriter Property and Casualty Insurance Edition* 77 (December 7, 1973): 27.

Krishnan, R. "Business Philosophy and Executive Responsibility." *Academy of Management Journal* 16 (December 1973): 658–669.

Kristol, Irving. "Ethics and the Corporation." *Wall Street Journal* 185 (April 16, 1975): 18.

"Kudos for Conscience." *Saturday Review of the Society* 1 (March 17, 1973): 60.
>   Examples of corporate responsibility.

Lawrence, Floyd G. "Whose Ethics Guide Business?" *Industry Week* 187 (October 27, 1975): 23–27+.
>   A discussion on the value of ethical codes of conduct in the corporation. "They make sense only if you make them a living document."

Lens, Sidney. "Moral Roots of the New Despair." *Christian Century* 92 (February 26, 1975): 192–196.

McCall, David B. "Profit Spur for Solving Social Ills." *Harvard Business Review* 51 (May-June 1973): 46–56.

McMahon, Thomas. "Classroom Ethics: A Survey of Business School Courses." *Business and Society Review* 14 (Summer 1975): 21–23.
>   A summary of a careful and illuminating research project.

McNulty, Nancy G. "And Now, Professional Codes for the Practice of Management." *Conference Board Record* 12 (April 1975): 21–24.

Mayer, Lawrence A. "A Large Question About Large Corporations." *Fortune* (May 1972): 185+.

Melloan, George. "Business Morality and Its Vocal Critics." *Wall Street Journal* 178 (August 26, 1971): 10.

Meltzer, T. S. "Are Proposed Kickback Regulations an Unwarranted Extension of the Code?" *Journal of Taxation* 38 (March 1973): 166–169.

Miller, Andrew. "Corporations: Public Servants or Private Outlaws?" *Christianity and Crisis* 32 (February 7, 1972): 4–8.

"Minding the Corporate Conscience 1974." *Economic Priorities Report* 5 (1974): 3–72.

Morgenson, Donald F. "White Collar Crime and the Violation of Trust." *Personnel Journal* 54 (March 1975): 154, 176.

Moskowitz, Milton. "Conscientious Corporations: A Record." *Sloan Management Review* 13 (Fall 1971): 25–30.

Mueller, Willard F. "The Rising Economic Concentration in America: Reciprocity, Conglomeration, and the New American 'Zaibatsu' System." *Antitrust and Economics Review* (Spring 1971): 15–50.

Myers, M. Scott. "The Human Factor in Management Systems." *California Management Review* 14 (Fall 1971): 5–10.

Myers, S. C. "A Simple Model of Firm Behavior Under Regulation and Uncertainty." *The Bell Journal of Economics and Management Science* (Spring 1973): 304–315.

Nagel, Thomas. "Reason and National Goals: National Resource Allocation Cannot Be Rational if It Is Not Ethical." *Science* 177 (September 1, 1972): 766–770.

"New Style in Public Enemies—The White Collar Criminal." *U.S. News and World Report* 74 (March 12, 1973): 53–55.

Newstrom, John W. and William A. Ruch. "Ethics of Management and the Management of Ethics." *MSU Business Topics* 23 (Winter 1975): 29–37.
   Executives ought to and can raise standards—the pay-off is clear. It is good business to be ethical.

Nolan, James. "FBI Agent Accountants Intensify Campaign Against 'White Collar' Crime." *Journal of Accountancy* 138 (October 1974): 26+.

Noll, Lawrence W. "Ethics and the Businessman." *Akron Business and Economic Review* 4 (Fall 1973): 45–48.

Nolting, Frederick E. "Watergate May Turn Out to Be a Catharsis to American Business." *U.S. News and World Report* 77 (August 26, 1974): 67–69.

Oliver, Bernard M. "Toward a New Morality." *IEEE Spectrum* 9 (January 1972): 52–54.
   It is time that science, having destroyed the religious basis for morality, accepted the obligation to provide a new and rational basis for human behavior—a code of ethics concerned with man's needs on earth, not his rewards in heaven.

O'Neill, Eileen Cramer. "Creating and Promoting a Code of Ethics." *Association Management* (November 1972): 44+.

Purcell, Theodore V. "A Practical Guide to Ethics in Business." *Business and Society Review* 13 (Spring 1975): 43–50.
   A definition of applied business ethics with illustrations of how an ethicist works.

Rockefeller, Rodman C. "The Role of Business—Doing Well or Doing Good." *Looking Ahead* 20 (September 1972): 1–5.

Ruch, W. A. and J. W. Newstrom. "How Unethical Are We?" *Supervisory Management* 20 (November 1975): 16–21.

Scott, Gordon. "Viewpoint—The Other Ethics." *The Personnel Administrator* 20 (April 1975): 14.
   A short editorial introducing the various articles in this issue by noting the difference between personal morality and a societal morality of 'Fairness'.

Shields, J. O. "Corporate Conscience: Giving a Damn." *Administrative Management* 32 (November 1971): 66–67.

Simons, G. "Ethics For Personnel Firms." *The Canadian Personnel and Industrial Relations Journal* (September 1973): 24+.

Singer, Peter. "Altruism and Commerce." *Philosophy and Public Affairs* 2 (Spring 1973): 312–320.

Stackhouse, Max L. "Countering the Military-Industrial Complex: A New Ethic for Large Scale Institutions." *Christianity & Crisis* 31 (February 22, 1971): 14–22.

"Stiffer Rules for Business Ethics." *Business Week* (March 30, 1974): 87–89.

Sturm, Douglas. "Corporations, Constitutions, and Covenants: On Forms of Human Relation and the Problem of Legitimacy." *Journal of the American Academy of Religion* (September 1973): 331–354.
   An erudite essay by a social ethicist speaking to the issue of corporate legitimacy.

Thompson, D. B. "Looking Beyond Today's Profits." *Industry Week* 176 (February 5, 1973): 40-41+.

Trowbridge, Alexander B. "Business." *Saturday Review* (November 1, 1975): 18–20.
   Corporate businessmen have engaged in unethical behavior.

Vandivier, Kermit W. "A Case of Corporate Corruption." *Progressive* 34 (November 1970): 23–26.

Walker, Frederick W., Jr. "Productivity, Profits and Business Ethics." *SAM Advanced Management Journal* 38 (July 1973): 2–8.

Walter, Kenneth Dale. "Freedom of Speech in Modern Corporations." Doctoral Dissertation, University of California, Berkeley, 1972.

"Watergating on Main Street." (A symposium on professional ethics). *Saturday Review* (November 1975): 10–27.
    A panel of experts assess the ethics of business managers, doctors, lawyers, journalists, educators and politicians.

Ways, Max. "Business Faces Growing Pressures to Behave Better." *Fortune* (May 1974): 192–195; 310, 314, 316, 319, 320.
    The barefoot morality of our past is not enough to meet the complex business ethical issues of our day, argues the author.

Webley, Simon. "Business Policy and Business Ethics." *Journal of Business Policy* 3 (Spring 1973): 3–10.

Weintraub, Sidney, ed. "Income Inequality." *The Annals of the American Academy of Political and Social Science* 409 (September 1973): 111–245.
    The entire volume is devoted to the matter of earnings discrepancies in the United States. This lively and practical discussion is carried on by such scholars as Walter Weisskopf, Kenneth Boulding, and Mary Townsend Hamilton, et al.

Whitaker, John. "The Supremacy of the Business Ethic." *Business and Society Review/Innovation* 10 (Summer 1974): 91–96.
    The values of countervailing power for business and society are discussed. The author explicates many changes that have already taken place in business as a result of societal pressures.

Wilkens, Paul. "The Case for Ethical Absolutes." *Business and Society Review* 13 (Spring 1975): 61–63.
    The author thinks it is both possible and necessary to develop uniform and absolute codes of conduct in business.

Wylie, F. W. "Common Code of Ethics." *Public Relations Journal* 30 (February 1974): 14–15.

Zonana, Victor F. "Bribery and Slush Spur Ethics Courses at Business Schools." *Wall Street Journal* (July 8, 1975).

Business Ethics and Functional Areas
of Management

Business Ethics and Functional Areas
of Management

Accounting

Books

American Institute of Certified Public Accountants. *AICPA PROFESSIONAL STANDARDS*. Chicago: Commerce Clearing House, 1974.

American Institute of Certified Public Accountants. *Code of Professional Ethics: Concepts of Professional Ethics, Rules of Conduct, Interpretations of Rules of Conduct*. New York, 1974.

Briloff, Abraham. *Unaccountable Accounting*. New York: Harper & Row, 1972.

Causey, Denzil Y. *Duties and Liabilities of Public Accountants*. Austin: University of Texas, Bureau of Business Research, 1973.

Estes, Ralph W. *Accounting and Society*. Los Angeles: Melville Publishing Company, 1973.

Livingstone, John Leslie and Sanford C. Gunn. *Accounting for Social Goals: Budgeting and Analysis of Nonmarket Projects*. New York: Harper & Row Publishers, Inc., 1974.

McGrath, Phyllis and Francis Walsh, Jr. *Disclosure of Financial Forecasts to Security Analysts and the Public*. New York: Conference Board, 1973.

Seidler, Lee J. *Social Accounting: Theory, Issues and Cases*. New York: John Wiley and Sons. Incorporated, 1975.

Vangermeersch, Richard G. *Accounting: Socially Responsible and Socially Relevant*. New York: Harper & Row Publishers, Inc., 1972.

Articles

"The Accountants' Last Chance: If the New Board Fizzles, the Rules Will Be Set by Government Edict." *Business Week* (March 31, 1973): 91–92.

"Accounting: A Crisis over Fuller Disclosure." *Business Week* (April 22, 1972): 54–60.

"AICPA Ethics Division Answers Members' Queries on Ethics Code." *Journal of Accountancy* 138 (July 1974): 61–62.

"AICPA Ethics Rulings." *Journal of Accountacy* 140 (September 1975): 86.

"AICPA MAS Committee Issues Exposure Drafts of Standards for Practice and Preparation of Financial Forecasts." *Management Advisor* 11 (May 1974): 9–10.

Andrews, Frederick. "Inside and Outside: Why Didn't Auditors Find Something Wrong with Equity Funding?" *Wall Street Journal* 181 (May 4, 1973): 45–54.

"Annual Reports Bare Long-Hidden Facts." *Business Week* (April 3, 1971): 65–66.

Anreder, S. S. "Called to Account: Accountants Are Striving to Close the Credibility GAAP." *Barron's* 52 (October 2, 1972): 3+.

Armstrong, Marshall S. "Corporate Accountability: A Challenge to Business." *The Conference Board Record* 8 (August 1971): 28–31.

Armstrong, Marshall S. "Establishing Accounting Standards in a Free Society." *National Public Accountant* 19 (December 1974): 16–21.

Armstrong, Marshall S. "Financial Reporting: Will Washington Listen to the Private Sector?" *Financial Executive* 42 (March 1974): 52–56+.

"Auditors-Guardians of Morals?" *The CPA* 45 (September 1975): 9–10.

Austin, Richard H. "CPA's Social, Civic and Political Responsibilities." *The Journal of Accountancy* 132 (December 1971): 64–66.

Baker, Richard T. "Why Aren't We Solving Our Problems in Accounting Principles?" *Financial Executive* 40 (January 1972): 14–17.

Balz, Daniel J. "Coalition Seeks to Force Large Firms to Open Books and Show Price Decisions." *National Journal* 5 (June 16, 1973): 859–865.

Bedford, Norton M. "Corporate Accountability." *Management Accounting* 55 (November 1973): 41–44.

Bedingfield, J. P. and Steven E. Loeb. "Attitudes of Professors Toward Accounting Ethics." *Accounting Review* 48 (July 1973): 603–605.

Benjamin, James J. and Vincent C. Brenner. "Public Disclosure for CPA Firm." *Financial Executive* (August 1975): 37–41.

Benston, George J. "Accountants' Integrity and Financial Reporting." *Financial Executive* (August 1975): 10–14.

Beresford, D. R. "How Companies Are Reporting Social Performance." Management Accounting 56 (August 1974): 41–44.

Beyer, Robert. "Pilots of Social Progress." *Management Accounting* 54 (July 1972): 11–15.
Discusses corporate social responsibility and the role that business could and should play in finding solutions to the problems of society.

Biagioni, Louis F. "Roles and Rules for Accountants." *Business Horizons* 18 (February 1975): 67–75.
Users of accounting reports have a right to expect integrity. An understanding of users' reactions to information would help accountants develop rules of measurement and disclosure.

Bibbero, Richard V. "Tips on Embezzlement." *National Public Accountant* 16 (May 1971): 22–24+.

Bock, Betty. "Competition Through the Looking Glass." *Conference Board Record* 10 (March 1973): 11–17.
On disclosure perils and possibilities.

Bows, Albert J., Jr. "Establishment of Financial Accounting Standards." *Management Accounting* 54 (December 1972): 9—12+.
Each of the Big Eight Accounting Firms . . . . must find new channels of input to the financial accounting standards board.

Brenner, V. C. "Some Observations on Student Values and Their Implications for Accounting Education." *Accounting Review* 48 (July 1973): 605–608.

Briloff, Abraham J. Accounting: A Learned Profession Succeeds with Pens Where Surgeons Fail." *Commercial and Financial Chronicle* 219 (June 24, 1974): 11–12+.

Briloff, Abraham J. "Bill of Impeachment Against Accountants." *Commercial and Financial Chronicle* 220 (January 13, 1975): 9+.

Briloff, Abraham J. "Corporate Financial Reporting Quagmire." *Commercial and Financial Chronicle* 215 (January 13, 1972: 125+.

Briloff, Abraham J. "Prescription for Change." Management Accounting 56 (July 1974): 63–65+.
Unless there is something of a major moral renaissance in the totality of our existence we are just not going to make it as a complex civilization.

Briloff, Abraham J. "Six Flags at Half-Mast? Great Southwest Corp. Hasn't Exactly Raised Accounting Standards." *Barron's* 51 (January 11, 1971): 5+.
Another harsh evaluation.

Brown, W. Warren. "Businessman Talks about Accounting Standards." *Financial Executive* 41 (November 1973): 56–58+.

Buckley, John W. "Accounting Principles and the Social Ethic." *Financial Executive* 39 (October 1971): 32–34+.

Burton, John C. "A Report from the Symposium on Ethics in Corporate Financial Reporting." *Journal of Commercial Bank Lending* 54 (January 1972): 51–58.

Carmichael, Douglas R. "Meeting the Expectations of the Young Accountant." *The Journal of Accountancy* 131 (May 1971): 71–73.

Casey, William J. "Credibility and Cleavage Problems of the Accounting Profession." *Accounting Review* 46 (April 1971): 387–389.

Chambers, Raymond J. "Accounting Principles or Accounting Policies?" *Journal of Accountancy* 135 (May 1973): 48–53.

Chambers, Raymond J. "Anguish of Accountants." *Journal of Accountancy* 133 (March 1972): 68–74.

Churchill, N. C. "Toward a Theory for Social Accounting." *Sloan Management Review* 15 (September 1974): 1–17.

Cotlett, G. R. "Relationship of Auditing Standards to Detection of Fraud." *The CPA Journal* 45 (April 1975): 13–21.

Cruse, R. B. "Ethics for the CPA in Industry." *Journal of Accountancy* 139 (June 1975): 71–73.

Demski, J. S. "General Impossibility of Normative Accounting Standards." *Accounting Review* 48 (October 1973): 718–723.

Dominiak, G. F. and J. G. Louderback, 3d. "Present Fairly and Generally Accepted Accounting Principles." *The CPA Journal* 42 (January 1972): 45–49.

Earle, Victor M., III. "Accountants on Trial in the Theatre of the Absurd." *Fortune* 85 (May 1972): 227–228+.

Fortunato, F. A. "Quest for Fairness in Accounting." *Management Accounting* 53 (January 1972): 15–18.

Fox, Gary A. "The Accounting Principles Board—Victim or Villain?" *Miami Business Review* 44 (February 1973): 1–4.

Francia, A. J. and R. H. Strawser. "Perceptions of Financial Reporting Practices by Accounting Educators. An Empirical Study." *Accounting Review* 46 (April 1971): 380–384.

Frishkoff, Paul. "Consistency in Auditing and APB Opinion No. 20." *Journal of Accountancy* 134 (August 1972): 64–70.

Graese, C. E. "Ethics Division Rulings on Past Due Billings and Bank Directorships." *Journal of Accountancy* 139 (February 1975): 81–84.

Guy, D. M. "Proposed Statement of Audit Responsibility for Projected Financial Statements." *The CPA Journal* 42 (December 1972): 1009–1011+.

Harris, Arthur F. M. "New Accounting Problems Ahead for Associations." *Association Management* 23 (July 1971): 36–41.

Hartley, Ronald V. and Timothy L. Ross. "MAS and Audit Independence: An Image Problem." *Journal of Accountancy* 134 (November 1972): 42–51.

Henderson, J. G. "What Is Happening to Professional Conduct?" *The CPA Journal* 45 (May 1975): 7–8.

Hershman, Arlene. "The War over Corporate Fraud [Auditors' Responsibility]." *Dun's* 104 (November 1974): 51–55.
    Can investors and the SEC make accountants pay the bill? Just how responsible are auditors to their clients and the public—how much will they have to reveal?

Higgins, Thomas G. and Wallace E. Olson. "Restating the Ethics Code: A Decision for the Times." *The Journal of Accountancy* 133 (March 1972): 33–39.

Horngren, Charles T. "Accounting Principles: Private or Public Sector?" *Journal of Accountancy* 133 (May 1972): 37–41.

"Interpretations of Rules 101 and 202 of the Code of Professional Ethics." *Journal of Accountancy* 139 (January 1975): 72–73.

"Interpretations of Rules 501 and 502 of the Code of Professional Ethics." *Journal of Accountancy* 139 (April 1975): 66-68.

Kapnick, Harvey. "Public Accountability—A Challenge for the Accounting Profession." *The CPA Journal* 44 (October 1974): 29–31+.

Kapnick, Harvey. "Responsibilities of the Accounting Profession." *Management Accounting* 53 (March 1972): 21–24.
    The view is taken that the ability of public accountants to perform useful services for society will determine whether they will continue to be an effective and vigorous part of our free-enterprise system.

Kastenholz, Francis E. "Accountant's View of Corporate Responsibility." *Financial Executive* 42 (April 1974): 68–70+.

Kemp, P. S. "Further Look at Fairness in Accounting." *Management Accounting* 54 (January 1973): 15–16+.

Knortz, Herbert C. "Credibility of Accounting Principles." *The Conference Board Record* 8 (April 1971): 33–38.

Lambert, Joyce C. "Proposed Code of Professional Conduct." *Management Accounting* 55 (February 1974): 19–22.
    This is an effort to develop a code of professional conduct for management accountants beginning with the ethical philosophy of St. Thomas Aquinas as a philosophical base. Includes a survey of responses on the proposed code.

Leone, R. L. "Accountant's Role in a Controlled Society." *Management Advisor* 9 (September 1972): 51–54.

Levine, H. "Social Debt of Government Accountants." *The Office* 79 (January 1974): 114.

Limbert, G. Christian, Jr. "Evaluating Federal Poverty Programs:

Can the Auditor's Attest Function Be Extended to Making Such Evaluations?" *Price Waterhouse Review* 16 (Summer/Autumn 1971): 50–59.

Linowes, David F. "Accountant's Enlarged Professional Responsibilities." *Journal of Accountancy* 135 (February 1973): 47–51.

Linowes, David F. "Accounting Profession and Social Progress." *Journal of Accountancy* 136 (July 1973): 32–40.

Linowes, David F. "Social Responsibility of the Profession." *Journal of Accountancy* 131 (January 1971): 66–69.

Loeb, Stephen E. "Code of Ethics for CPA's in Industry: A Survey." *Journal of Accountancy* 132 (December 1971): 52–60.

Loeb, Stephen E. and Burt A. Leete. "Dual Practitioner: CPA, Lawyer or Both?" *Journal of Accountancy* 136 (August 1973): 57–63.

Loeb, Stephen E. "Enforcement of the Code of Ethics: A Survey." *Accounting Review* 47 (January 1972): 1–10.

Loeb, Stephen E. "Fee Splitting: An Old Rule with a New Look." *Journal of Accountancy* 140 (October 1975): 79–82.

Loeb, Stephen E. "Incompatible Occupations for CPA's—An Inquiry into Compliance." *New York Certified Public Accountant* 41 (June 1971): 433–437.

Loeb, Stephen E. "Survey of Ethical Behavior in the Accounting Profession." *Journal of Accounting Research* 9 (Autumn 1971): 287–306.

Loeb, Stephen E. and J. P. Bedingfield. "Teaching Accounting Ethics." *Accounting Review* 47 (October 1972): 811–813.

Lowes, B. and J. R. Sparkes. "Fitting Accounting to Social Goals." *Business Horizons* 17 (June 1974): 53–57.

Malinosky, A. T. and Carl M. Larson. "Is the Public Accountant Guilty of Benign Neglect Toward Small Businesses?" *National Public Accountant* 18 (June 1973): 18–19+.

Marlin, John Tepper. "Accounting for Pollution." *Journal of Accountancy* 135 (February 1973): 71–74.

Mautz, R. K. "Accounting Principles—How Can They Be Made More Authoritative?" *The CPA Journal* 43 (March 1973): 185–192.

Mobley, S. C. "Opportunities for Accountants in the Socio-Economic Area." *The CPA Journal* 43 (December 1973): 1050–1052.

Nash, J. "Accounting Practices Criticized." *Commercial and Financial Chronicle* 218 (November 26, 1973): 1553+.

Neuman, David. "Cost Accounting Standards: The CPA's Newest Challenge." *Federal Accountant* 20 (December 1971): 20–29.

Nolan, James. "Evolution of a Code of Ethics: Tom Higgins Was There." *The Journal of Accountancy* 133 (April 1972): 22–24.

Noonan, E. R. "1973 Accounting Principles—Evolution or Revolution?" *Journal of Commercial Bank Lending* 55 (January 1973): 19–27.

"Numbers Game: The Right to Know—or the Right to Nose?" *Forbes* 114 (August 1, 1974): 37–8.

O'Glove, Thornton and Robert Olstein. "What Accountants Don't Tell Us." *Dun's* 101 (April 1973): 121–122.
    Discusses the need to improve disclosure policies and suggests SEC appoint independent qualified certified financial analysts to evaluate the adequacy of the disclosure practices.

Oliphant, W. J. "Search for Accounting Principles." *Journal of Accountancy* Sup. 9 (1972): 93–98.

Pointer, Larry Gene. "Disclosing Corporate Tax Policy." *Journal of Accountancy* 136 (July 1973): 56–61.

"Report on the Symposium on Ethics in Corporate Financial Reporting (Seaview, N.J.) *Analysts Journal* 28 (January 1972): 49–53. Also in *Financial Executive* 40 (January 1972): 28–30+.

"Retention of Client's Records—Professional Ethics." *The CPA* 45 (July 1975): 53.

Roberts, Markley. "Corporate Secrecy and the Public Interest: A Labor View." *National Public Accountant* 18 (October 1973): 8–12.

Ross, Howard. "Is It Better to Be Precisely Wrong than Vaguely Right?" *Financial Executive* 39 (June 1971): 8–12.

Saxe, E. "Accountants' Responsibility for Unaudited Financial Statements." *The New York Certified Public Accountant* 41 (June 1971): 419–423.

Seider, Lee J. "Accountant: Account for Thyself." *Journal of Accountancy* 135 (June 1973): 38–43.

Shapiro, Leslie S. "The Importance of Being Ethical." *National Public Accountant* 17 (February 1974): 14–19.

Siegel, Joel and Patrick O'Driscoll. "Accounting: Its Social Implications." *National Public Accountant* 20 (March 1975): 15–19.

Skadden, Donald H. "Accounting Principles: Where Are They Leading?" *University of Michigan Business Review* 26 (September 1974): 25–32.

Smith, W. A. "Revised AICPA Rules of Conduct—To Serve the Public Interest." *The CPA Journal* 43 (November 1973): 963–968.

"Some Further Comments on Fair Value Accounting." *Financial Executive* 41 (January 1973): 52–54+.

Sommer, A. A., Jr. "Neglected Dimension of Financial Reporting." *Journal of Accountancy* 137 (April 1974): 71–74.

Sorensen, James E., John Grant Rhode and Edward E. Lawler, III. "Generation Gap in Public Accountancy." *Journal of Accountancy* 136 (December 1973): 42–50.

Stabler, Charles N. "Juggling the Books: Accounting Rules for Lease Transactions May be Tightened, Causing Woes for Firms." *Wall Street Journal* 178 (October 14, 1971): 34.

Stabler, Charles N. "Revelations: What Should Lawyers Tell Accountants About Legal Problems." *The Wall Street Journal* 183 (February 27, 1974): 1+.

Weston, Frank T. "Prepare for the Financial Accounting Revolution." *Harvard Business Review* 52 (September 1974): 6–8+.
    An outline and discussion of changes that will occur within financial accounting—and the role of the corporate manager in anticipating these changes.

"When Audit Rules Clash with Legal Ethics." *Business Week* (April 14, 1975): 72.

"Why Accountants Need to Tell a Fuller Story." *Business Week* (February 6, 1971): 86–87.

Advertising

Books

Barmash, Isadore. *The World Is Full of It; How We Are Oversold, Over-influenced, and Overwhelmed by the Communications Manipulators.* New York: Delacorte Press, 1974.

Brozen, Yale, ed. *Advertising and Society.* New York: New York University Press, 1974.

Buxton, Edward. *Promise Them Anything; The Inside Story of the Madison Avenue Power Struggle.* New York: Stein and Day, 1972.

Divita, Salvatore F. *Advertising and the Public Interest.* Chicago: American Marketing Association, 1974.

Greyser, Stephen A. *Cases in Advertising and Communications Management.* Englewood Cliffs, New Jersey: Prentice-Hall, 1972.

Howard, John A. and James Hulbert. *Advertising and the Public Interest; A Staff Report to the Federal Trade Commission.* New York, 1973.

Inglis, Fred. *The Imagery of Power: A Critique of Advertising.* London: Heinemann, 1972.

James, Don L. *Youth, Media, and Advertising.* Austin: Austin Bureau of Business Research, Graduate School of Business, University of Texas, 1971.

Karp, Robert E., ed. *Issues in Marketing.* New York: MSS Information Corporation, 1974.

Key, Wilson Bryan. *Subliminal Seduction: Ad Media's Manipulation of a Not So Innocent America.* Englewood Cliffs, New Jersey: Prentice Hall, 1973.

Kintner, Earl W. *A Primer on the Law of Deceptive Practices; A Guide for the Businessman.* New York: Macmillan, 1971.

Kuhns, William. *The Information Explosion.* Camden, New Jersey: T. Nelson, 1971.

Langholz Leymore, Varda. *Hidden Myths: Structure & Symbolism in Advertising.* London: Heinemann Educational, 1975.

Lois, George and Bill Pitts. *George, Be Careful; A Greek Florist's Kid in the Roughhouse World of Advertising.* New York: Saturday Review Press, 1972.

Lucas, John T. and Richard Gurman. *Truth in Advertising.* New York: American Management Association, 1972.
An AMA research report in response to increasing consumer demands for fair and honest treatment.

Mertes, John E. *Corporate Communications: The Promotional View.* Norman: Bureau for Business and Economic Research, University of Oklahoma, 1972.

Millum, Trevor. *Images of Woman: Advertising in Women's Magazines.* Totowa, New Jersey: Rowman and Littlefield, 1975.

Milton, Shirley F. *Advertising for Modern Retailers; Making It Work in a Consumer World.* New York: Fairchild Publications, 1974.

Moskin, J. Robert, ed. *The Case for Advertising.* New York: American Association of Advertising Agencies, 1973.

Myers, John G. *Social Issues in Advertising.* New York: AAAA Educational Foundation, Inc., 1971.

The New FTC Approach to Advertising Regulation. Jerrold G. Van-Cise and Marcus Mattson, chairmen. New York: Practising Law Institute, 1971.

Nicholl, David Shelly. *Advertising; Its Purpose, Principles and Practice.* London: Macdonald & Evans, 1973.

Nicosia, Francesco M., ed. *Advertising, Management, and Society: A Business Point of View.* New York: McGraw Hill, 1974.

Preston, Ivan L. *The Great American Blow-up: Puffery in Advertising and Selling.* Madison: University of Wisconsin Press, 1975.

Schrank, Jeffrey. *Deception Detection.* Beacon Press, 1975.
Psychological aspects.

Schwartz, Tony. *The Responsive Chord.* 1st ed. Garden City, New York: Anchor Press, 1973.
Psychological and social aspects of communication in advertising.

Stridsberg, Albert B. *Effective Advertising Self-Regulation: A Survey of Current World Practice and Analysis of International Patterns.* New York: International Advertising Association, 1974.

29

Stuart, Fredrick, ed. *Consumer Protection from Deceptive Advertising.* Hempstead, New York: Hofstra University, 1974.

Truth in Advertising: A Symposium of the Toronto School of Theology, University of Toronto. Toronto, Fitzhenry & Whiteside; New York: Harper & Row, 1972.

Whiteside, Thomas. *Selling Death; Cigarette Advertising and Public Health.* New York: Liveright, 1971.

Wight, Robin. *The Day the Pigs Refused to Be Driven to Market; Advertising and Consumer Revolution.* London: Hart-Davis, Mac-Gibbon Ltd., 1972.

Wright, John S. and John E. Mertes, eds. *Advertising's Role in Society.* St. Paul: West Publishing Company, 1974.

Articles

Achenbaum, A. A. "Advertising Doesn't Manipulate Consumers." *Journal of Advertising Research* 12 (April 1972): 3–13.

"Adman Battles Society's Ills." *Business Week* (September 11, 1971): 108+.
A report on how one agency focuses its creative talent on social cause advertising.

"Admen Set Up Their Own Watchdog." *Business Week* (June 12, 1971): 56.

"Ads on Church Page; You, Too, Can Chime In." *Editor & Publisher* 104 (January 23, 1971): 20.

"Advertising and Society." *Advertising Age* 44 (November 21, 1973): 156–183.
A discussion of social, political and educational roles.

"Advertising Code Still Developing." *Broadcasting* 80 (March 22, 1971): 58–59.

"Advertising Review Board—or Regulation by Government." *Editor & Publisher* 104 (February 6, 1971): 10.

Allan, Leslie and others. "Corporate Advertising and the Environment." *Economic Priorities Report* 2 (Sept./Oct. 1971): 1+.
This 39 p. report includes an analysis of environmental advertising of Ford, General Motors.

"Analgesic Ads: FTC's New Tack Is Case-by-Case." *Oil, Paint, and Drug Reporter* 199 (January 11, 1971): 7+.

"ANPA Aids Effort for Truthful Ads." *Editor & Publisher* 104 (April 24, 1971): 16a+.

Armstrong, Gary M. and Frederick A. Russ. "Detecting Deception in Advertising." *Michigan State University Business Topics* 23 (Spring 1975): 21–31.

Bell, Howard H. "Self-Regulation by the Advertising Industry." *California Management Review* 16 (Spring 1974): 58–63.

"Blacks in Ads Are Noted, But That's About All." *Editor & Publisher* 104 (January 9, 1971): 50.

Block, Carl E. "White Backlash to Negro Ads: Fact or Fantasy?" *Journalism Quarterly* 49 (Summer 1972): 258–262.

"Business Advisors Ask Less Government Restraints on Ads." *Advertising Age* 43 (November 13, 1972): 2+.

"California, Oklahoma Take Action Against National Home Life Ad." *The National Underwriter* (Life & Health Insurance Edition) 76 (May 6, 1972): 2.

Capitman, William G. "Morality in Advertising—A Public Imperative." *Business Topics* 19 (Spring 1971): 21-26.

Capitman, William G. "The Selling of the American Public." *Business & Society Review* (Summer 1972):42–46.
Like its clients, the advertising industry is feeling pressure of social discontent; the public is questioning adman's world view.

Carpenter, James W. "Consumer Protection in Ohio Against False Advertising and Deceptive Practices." *Ohio State Law Journal* 32 (Winter 1971): 1–15.

"Cereal Critic Presents Advertising Code." *Food Processing* 32 (April 1971): 67.

"Code Board Present to Independents." *Broadcasting* 80 (May 31, 1971): 27-28.
On code compliance.

"Code Board Talks of Rules for Advertising Aimed at Young." *Broadcasting* 83 (October 23, 1972): 23–24.

"Code for Advertising Now in Sight." *Broadcasting* 80 (February 8, 1971): 22–24.

Cohen, Dorothy. "Surrogate Indicators and Deception in Advertising." *Journal of Marketing* 36 (July 1972): 10-15.

"Colorado Orders Full Pricing in Automobile Ads." *Editor & Publisher* 104 (May 8, 1971): 24.

"Consumerism: Home for Madison Avenue." *Sales Management* 107 (October 18, 1971): 35+.

Courtney, Alice E. and Lockeretz, Sarah W. "Woman's Place: An Analysis of the Roles Portrayed by Women in Magazine Advertisements." *Journal of Marketing Research* 8 (February 1971): 92–95.

Cudmore, Gordon D. and James G. McLeod. "Misleading Advertising: How High an Onus?" *Business Quarterly* 40 (Summer 1975): 65–71.

"Deceptive Advertising: Pressures for Change." *Congressional Quarterly Weekly Report* 30 (April 1, 1972): 727–730.

"Denenberg Hearings Zero In on Deceptive Health Insurance Ads." *The National Underwriter* (Life & Health Insurance Edition) 76 (February 26, 1972): 1+.

Dominick, Joseph R. and Gail E. Rauch. "The Image of Women in Network TV Commercials." *Journal of Broadcasting* 16 (Summer 1972): 259–265.

Ellman, Ira Mark. "And Now a Word Against Our Sponsor." *California Law Review* 60 (Fall 1972): 1416–1450.
An essay on extending the FTC's fairness doctrine to advertising.

Elson, R. and W. Sheridan. "Plug Your Social Consciousness In on the Big Broadcast Band." *Public Relations Journal* 27 (November 1971): 38–39+.

"Enzyme Syndets: Tone Down Claims, Soapers Ordered." *Oil, Paint, and Drug Reporter* 199 (March 8, 1971): 4.

"FTC to Take Over on Deceptive Ads?" *Broadcasting* 80 (February 15, 1971): 60–62.

"FTC Gets Tougher on Misleading Ads." *Business Week* (December 11, 1971): 35.

"FTC Tells Analgesic Makers: Stop Giving Agency Headache Due to Deceptive Advertising." *Chemical Marketing Reporter* 201 (April 24, 1972): 5+.

"FTC Zooms In on the Better Buys." *Business Week* (February 20, 1971): 20–21.

Gardner, David M. "Can Deceptive Advertising Be Measured." (June 1973): 22 pp. *Working Series in Marketing Research* No. 18 Dept. of Marketing Pennsylvania State University, University Park, Pennsylvania 16802.

Gardner, David M. "Deception in Advertising: A Conceptual Approach." *Journal of Marketing* 39 (January 1975): 40–46.

Gardner, David M. "Distraction Hypothesis in Marketing." *Journal of Advertising Research* 10 (August 1970): 41–44.

Gardner, Judy. "Attacks on Advertising Continue as Agencies Work on New Regulatory Policies." *National Journal* 4 (September 9, 1972): 1427–1436.

Gartner, Michael. "When 'Fairness' Gets Out of Hand." *Wall Street Journal* 178 (September 8, 1971): 16.
     Effect of the FCC Fairness Doctrine on various court decisions involving TV advertising.

Greenland, Leo. "Advertisers Must Stop Conning Consumers." *Harvard Business Review* 52 (July 1974): 18-20.

Greyser, Stephen A. "Advertising: Attacks and Counters." *Harvard Business Review* 50 (March/April 1972): 22–24.
     Toward identifying the current issues and resolving social effects of advertising through remedial actions.

Greyser, Stephen A., and Bonnie B. Reece. "Businessmen Look Hard at Advertising." *Harvard Business Review* 49 (May/June 1971): 18–20+.

Griffin, G. "Truth in Advertising—Does It Pay?" *Arts Magazine* 46 (December 1974): 58–61.

Grimes, Warren S. "Control of Advertising in the United States and Germany." *Harvard Law Review* 84 (June 1971): 1769–1800.

Gross, Alfred. "Cents-off: A Critical Promotion Tactic." *Michigan State University Business Topics* 19 (Spring 1971): 13–20.

Haefner, James E. and Steven E. Permut. "An Approach to the Evaluation of Deception in Television Advertising." *Journal of Advertising* 3 (Fall 1974): 40–44.

"Heading Them Off at the Pass: NAB TV Code Adopts Drug-ad Guidelines." *Broadcasting* 84 (February 26, 1973): 21–23.

Hentoff, Nat. "Would You Run This Ad?" *Business and Society Review* 14 (Summer 1975): 8–13.
    A comparative survey and comment.

"Home Furnishings Industry Sets Voluntary Guidelines." *Advertising Age* 45 (July 8, 1974): 62.

Howard, John A. and James Hulbert. "Advertising and the Public Interest." *Advertising Age* 44 (March 12, 1973): 4A–4B+.

Howard, John A. and James Hulbert. "Advertising and the Public Interest." *Crain Communications, Inc.* 96+2 pages.
    This is an analytical staff report to the FTC of the testimony and record of the Commission's hearings on modern advertising practices.

Howard, John A. and Spencer F. Tinkham. "A Framework for Understanding Social Criticism of Advertising." *Journal of Marketing* 35 (October 1971): 2–7.

"Housing Ad Guidelines Are Drafted." *Editor & Publisher* 104 (May 29, 1971): 16.

Knauer, Virginia H. "And Now a Word from the Consumer." *Public Relations Journal* 28 (December 1972): 6–7+.

Loevinger, Lee. "Attack on Advertising and the Goals of Regulations." *The Conference Board Record* 10 (January 1973): 23–28.

Lushbough, C. H. "Advertising: Consumer Information and Consumer Deception." *California Management Review* 16 (Spring 1974): 80–82.

MacGregor, James. "Coming Clean: Skeptical Consumers, Tough Regulators Spur a New Candor in Ads." *Wall Street Journal* 179 (January 12, 1972): 1+.

"Madison Avenue's Response to Its Critics." *Business Week* (June 10, 1972): 46–50.

34

A special report on agencies seeking to develop ads that are both effective and acceptable to consumerists.

Maggard, John P. and Gordon L. Wise. "The Role and Responsibilities of Advertising in a Decade of Challenge: Quo Vadis." *Miami Business Review* 44 (November 1972): 1–4.

Moskowitz, Daniel B. "FTC Testing Its Power." *Exchange* 32 (April 1971): 12–17.

Murphy, James A. "Advertising: A New Sense of Social Responsibility." *Bulletin of Business Research* 46 (September 1971): 4+.

"Nader Urges Industrial Admen to Share Talent for Public Good." *Industrial Marketing* 59 (August 1974): 10–12.

Nelson, R. "Cereals: Nutrition Doesn't Crackle or Pop." *Marketing/Communications* 299 (March 1971): 38–42.

"New Code in Sight for Advertising." *Broadcasting* 80 (May 24, 1971): 22+.

"New York Congressman Introduces Bill to Bar States from Prohibiting Rx Drug Price Ads." *American Druggist* 163 (March 8, 1971): 24.

"Pennsylvania Judge Orders Ads De-sexed." *Editor & Publisher* 104 (April 17, 1971): 72.

"Pennsylvania Rx Ad Ban Held Unconstitutional." *American Druggist* 163 (January 25, 1971): 15.

Permut, Steven Eli and James E. Haefner. "Exploring Deception and Puffery in Television Advertising." *Journal of the Academy of Marketing Sciences* 1 (Fall 1973): 156–166.

"Posting of Rx Prices OK in Massachusetts." *American Druggist* 163 (March 22, 1971): 24.

Powledge, Fred. "Judgement on Madison Avenue." *Money* 2 (September 1973): 82–84.
 In two years as its own policeman, the advertising business has brought quite a few national ads closer to the truth.

"Product Advertising and Consumer Safety." *Advertising Age* 45 (July 1, 1974): 47–50.

Reilly, John H., Jr. "A Welfare Critique of Advertising.: *American Journal of Economics and Sociology* 31 (July 1972): 283–293.

"Report Accuses Advertising Art of Superdome Contract Bribe." *Advertising Age* 46 (May 5, 1975): 30.

"Review Board to Publicize Censured Ads." *Editor & Publisher* 104 (May 29, 1971): 14.

Roberts, Churchill. "The Portrayal of Blacks on Network Television." *Journal of Broadcasting* 15 (Winter 1970-1971): 45–53.
On programs and in commercial advertisements over American television.

Robertson, Wyndham. "Tempest in Toyland." *Fortune* 85 (February 1972): 114–117+.
A discussion of toy marketing on television and the effects on children.

Sandman, Peter M. "Who Should Police Environmental Advertising." *Columbia Journalism Review* 10 (January/February 1972): 41–47.
Advertising attempting to capitalize on readers' concern with environmental pollution.

Scala, James R. "Advertising and Shared Monopoly in Consumer Goods Industries [United States]." *Columbia Journal of Law and Social Problems* 9 (Winter 1973): 241–278.

Settle, Robert B. and Linda L. Golden. "Attribution Theory and Advertiser Credibility." *Journal of Marketing Research* 11 (May 1974): 181–185.

Shafer, Ronald G. "The Whole Truth." *Wall Street Journal* 176 (November 12, 1970): 40.

Stuteville, John R. "Psychic Defenses Against High Fear Appeals: A Key Marketing Variable." *Journal of Marketing* 34 (April 1970): 39–45.

Stuteville, John R. "Sexually Polarized Products and Advertising Strategy.' *Journal of Retailing* 47 (Summer 1971): 3–13.

"Talking Up Self-Regulation to the Hill." *Broadcasting* 80 (June 14, 1971): 58–59.

Thain, Gerald J. "Consumer Protection: Advertising—the FTC Response." *Business Lawyer* 27 (April 1972): 891–906.

Thompson, Mayo J. "Advertising and the FTC." *Antitrust Law and Economics Review* 6 (November 4, 1973): 73–82.
Reflections on the role of information in a free-enterprise economy.

Tyson, I. W. "Tell Me Quick and Tell Me True." *Public Relations Journal* 30 (November 1974): 12–14.

"Two Guns Take Aim at Food Ads." *Broadcasting* 80 (February 22, 1971): 45–46.
Television and children.

"U.S. Firms Take Lead in Helping Minorities [Advertising Council's OMBE Involvement]" *Commerce Today* 1 (March 22, 1971): 14–17.

Walker, J., Jr. "Advertisers Ask Fairness in Consumerism Reports." *Editor & Publisher* 105 (March 25, 1972): 9.
American Association of Advertising Agencies Meeting.

Ward, Scott. "Kids' TV-Marketers on Hot Seat." *Harvard Business Review* 50 (July/August 1972): 16–18+.
This research evidence helps clarify burning consumerists' issue of children's TV advertising.

Wark, Lois G. "Criticism of Advertising Prompts Agency Crackdown, Industry Self-Regulation." *National Journal* 3 (August 7, 1971): 1633–1645.

Wasem, G. "Coming: More Regulation of Bank Advertising." *Bankers Monthly* 89 (September 1972): 17–19+.

"We Nominate for Oblivion Those Stupid, Hypocritical Corporate Ads." *Industrial Marketing* 56 (March 1971): 68–70+.

Weiss, E. B. "Advertising Meets Its Era of Social Accountability." *Advertising Age* 43 (October 23, 1973): 71–72+.

"What's A Remorseful Advertiser to Do?" *Sales Management* 105 (December 15, 1970): 40–41.

Wilkinson, J. B. and J. Barry Mason. "The Grocery Shopper and Food Specials: A Case of Subjective Deception?" *Journal of Consumer Affairs* 8 (Summer 1974): 30–36.

"Women Win Ruling for Sexless Ads." *Editor & Publisher* 105 (February 5, 1972): 38.

Worcester, Dale V. "Self-regulation in the Advertising Industry." *Pittsburgh Business Review* 40 (May 1970): 2–7.

Yankelovich, Daniel. "What New Life Styles Mean to Market Planners." *Marketing/Communications* 299 (June 1971): 38–45.

Employee Relations and Personnel Management

Books

Barkin, Solomon, ed. *Worker Militancy and Its Consequences, 1965–75: New Directions in Western Industrial Relations.* New York: Praeger Publishers, 1975.
Unions have had success in extending their rights and those of employees to participate in decision making on a broad range of subjects. Equity and freedom are increasing, according to the writers.

Braverman, Harry. *Labor and Monopoly Capital: The Degradation Work in the Twentieth Century.* New York: Monthly Review Press, 1975.

Caplan, Edwin H. and Stephen Landekich. *Human Resource Accounting: Past, Present and Future.* New York: National Association of Accountants, 1974.
Summary of the evolution of human resource accounting.

Davis, Louis, and A. Cherns. *The Quality of Working Life,* Vols. I and II. New York: Free Press, 1975.

Flamholtz, Eric. *Human Resource Accounting.* Encino, California: Dickenson Publishing Company, Inc., 1974.
Designed to be an introduction to human resource accounting.

Hinrichs, John R. *The Motivation Crises: Winding Down and Turning Off.* New York: Amacom (a division of the American Management Association), 1974.
Deals with quality of work in the present society and the interlocking pattern of development of the person, the job and the organization.

Legal Pitfalls in Firings and Layoffs. New York: Research Institute of America, 1975.

Rosow, Jerome M. *The Worker and the Job: Coping with Change.* Englewood Cliffs, N.J.: Prentice-Hall, 1974.

An exploration of the conflict between a society that is changing rapidly and a workplace that is not.

Seidenberg, Robert. *Corporate Wives—Corporate Casualties.* American Management Association, New York, 1973.

An illumination of problems regarding the stress and trauma experienced by wives. Some solutions are offered.

Tiefenthal, Rolf, ed. *Production: An International Appraisal of Contemporary Manufacturing Systems and the Changing Role of the Worker.* New York: Halsted Press, 1975.

The book shows how a firm can alter production organization so as to meet human needs and to integrate those needs with economic objectives.

Articles

Barrett, F. D. "Tomorrow's Management: Creative and Participative." *The Futurist* (February 1971): 12–13.

Beck, Ross. "Can the Production Line Be Humanized." *MSU Business Topics* (Autumn 1974): 27–36.

Berlo, David K. "Morality or Ethics? Two Approaches to Organizational Control." *Management Review* 64 (August 1975): 43–46.

Blum, James D. "Accounting for Human Resources, Another Accounting Alternative." *Business and Economic Dimensions* 10 (January/ February 1974): 1–9.

Boggs, M. D. and J. Ellenberger. "Worker Exploitation Dons a New Face in Haiti." *American Federationist* 80 (January 1973): 17–24.

Bolinder, Erik and Gideon Gerhardsson. "A Better Environment for the Worker." *International Labor Review* 105 (June 1972): 495–505.

Boyd, T. D. "Involvement Corps Matches Corporate Employees to Social Needs." *Management Review* 63 (June 1974): 20–24.

Castell, J. R. "Do You Want Dignity or Dividends?" [City National, Columbus, Ohio] *Banking* 63 (May 1971): 30–33.

Cross, Theodore and Paul London. "It Makes a Difference Where You Bank Your Money." *Business and Society Review/Innovation* (Winter 1973/1974): 22–31.

About employment practices of various New York banks in the area of employment of women and minorities.

Davis, Keith. "A Law of Diminishing Returns in Organizational Behavior." *Personnel Journal* 54 (December 1975): 616–619.

Concern for people and managerial autonomy is desirable up to a point of diminishing returns.

Deans, Ralph C. "Productivity and the New Work Ethic." *Editorial Research Reports* (April 19, 1972): 293–310.

Denzler, Richard D. "People and Productivity: Do They Still Equal Pay and Profits?" *Personnel Journal* 53 (January 1974): 59–63.

A discussion of the Protestant work ethic in the context of job enrichment theories.

Ellis, H. "When Top Executives Start to Depreciate." *Director* 25 (March 1973): 358–360.

England, George W. "Personal Value Systems of Managers—So What?" *The Personnel Administrator* 20 (April 1975): 20–23.

What is the relationship between personal values and managerial functioning? A short answer with some empirical data given.

Flamholtz, Eric. "Model for Human Resource Valuation: A Scholastic Process with Service Rewards." *Accounting Review* 46 (April 1971): 253–267.

Fleming, Sandra. "ERISA and the Employee's Right to Know." *Personnel Journal* 54 (June 1975): 346–349.

Knowledge of rights and obligations is what ERISA is all about. A discussion of the obligations of firms for informing employees (beyond the letter of the law) of their retirement benefits.

French, Gary L. "An Examination of Human Resource Accounting." *Business and Economic Dimensions* 10 (January/February 1974): 1–9.

Fulmer, Robert M. and William Fulmer. "Providing Equal Opportunities for Promotion." *Personnel Journal* 53 (July 1974): 491–497.

An examination and comparison of major selection methods for promotion.

Gambling, T. E. "Human Resource Accounting." *Moorgate and Wall Street* (Spring 1975): 39–48.

Gill, Kathleen Doyle. "Employee Communications and ERISA." *Personnel Administrator* 20 (May 1975): 23–26.
Specific guidelines are drawn up for proper employee communications.

Higgins, James M. "The Complicated Process of Establishing Goals for Equal Employment." *Personnel Journal* 54 (December 1975): 631–636.
An examination of problems associated with confusing and conflicting guidelines with some solutions for coping.

Lazer, Robert I. "Behavior Modification as a Managerial Technique." *The Conference Board Record* 12 (January 1975): 22–25.

Lens, Sidney. "Partners: Labor and the CIA." *Progressive* 39 (February 1975): 35–39.
The AFL-CIO is heavily involved in foreign intrigue without knowledge of rank and file.

Likert, Rensis and William C. Pyle. "Human Resource Accounting: An Organizational Approach." *Financial Analysts Journal* (January/February 1971).

McRae, Thomas W. "Human Resource Accounting as a Management Tool." *Journal of Accountancy* 138 (August 1974): 32–38.

Marcus, B. H. "Minority-Group Managers: An Experiment In Training." *Personnel* 48 (March 1971): 28–35.

"New Twist to People Accounting." *Business Week* (October 21, 1972): 67–68.

Newell, G. E. "Should Humans Be Reported as Assets?" *Management Accounting* 54 (December 1972): 13–16.

Newstrom, John W. "Self Actualization: An Emerging Employee Need." *The Personnel Administrator* 20 (April 1975): 31–32.
The contemporary concept of self-actualizing work is gaining more importance with present employees. Many consider it a right, not an ideal, says the author.

Oates, D. "Recognizing the Value of People." *International Management* 28 (March 1973): 36–39.

Phillips, C. "Company Secrets: Apex Chief Issues Leak Warning." *Industrial Management* 2 (September 1972): 45–47.
Concerning wage negotiations.

Pittman, C. R. "Organizational Behavior and the Management Accountant." *Management Accounting* 55 (July 1973): 25–28.

"Privacy, Polygraphs, and Employment." *United States Senate Committee on the Judiciary. Subcommittee on Constitutional Rights.* 93rd Congress 2nd Session.
The use of lie detectors on employees present and prospective.

Ranck, Lee. "Corporation of the Future." *Engage/Social Action* 2 (September 1974): 26–39.
The article reports on an insurance brokerage and administration firm (International Group Plans, Inc.) which focuses on employee power and "maximizing humaness."

Rein, Martin and Peter Marris. "Equality, Inflation and Wage Control." *Challenge* (March-April 1975): 42–50.

"Report of the Committee on Human Resource Accounting." *Accounting Review* 218 (1973): 169–185.

Roche, William J. and Niel L. Mackinnon. "Motivating People with More Meaningful Work." *Harvard Business Review* 49 (May 1971): 98.

Rouse, Victor W. "The Frustrated Black Worker." *Business Horizons* 14 (April 1971): 27–30.

Seashore, Stanley E. "Job Satisfaction as an Indicator of the Quality of Employment." *Social Indicators Research* 1 (September 1974): 135–168.
Value perspectives of employers and society should be stressed.

Sher, George. "Justifying Reverse Discrimination in Employment." *Philosophy and Public Affairs* 4 (Winter 1975): 159–170.
The point of reverse discrimination is to compensate for competitive disadvantages.

Silverman, Robert Stephen and D. A. Heming. "Exit the Organization Man: Enter the Professional Person." *Personnel Journal* 54 (March 1975): 146–148.
Increasing professionalism, individual stress on self actualization and a sense of creativity mark the new manager.

Singer, Henry A. "Human Values and Leadership." *Business Horizons* 18 (August 1975): 85–88.

"Special Issue on the Treatment of Human Resources in the National Accounts." *Review of Income and Wealth* 20 (December 1974): 439–514.

Stone, F. "Investment in Human Resources at AT&T." *Management Review* 61 (October 1972): 23–27.

Tavernier, G. "Would You Hire an Ex-prisoner?" *International Management* 29 (December 1974): 34–37+.

Weiss, M. "Accounting for Human Resources." *Management Review* 62 (March 1973): 58–60.

Weiss, M. "Human Resource Accounting—A Neglected Area." *The CPA Journal* 42 (September 1972): 735–743.

Weiss, M. "Where Human Resources Accounting Stands Today." *Administrative Management* 33 (November 1972): 43–48.

Finance

Books

Baruch, Hurd. *Wall Street: Security Risk.* Washington, D.C.: Acropolis Books, 1971.
Big Eight accounting firms are judged wanting in this study of the 1970 Trauma on Wall Street when Louis J. Lefkowitz charged auditors with gross violations of acceptable accounting practices.

Block, Stanley and Samuel Correnti. *Psyche, Sex, and Stocks: The Psychodynamic Key to Beating the Market.* Bridgewaters, New York: Windsor Books, 1973.

Burton, John C., ed. *Corporate Financial Reporting: Ethical and Other Problems.* Absecon, New Jersey: American Institute of Certified Public Accountants, 1972.

Elias, Christopher. *Fleecing the Lambs.* Chicago: Regnery, 1971.
The focus is on some auditors in this critical muckraking analysis of the "Back Office Mess in Wall Street."

Loeb, Gerald M. *The Battle for Stock Market Profits (Not the Way It's Taught at Harvard Business School)*. New York: Simon and Schuster, 1971.

Margolius, Sidney K. *The Innocent Investor and the Shaky Ground Floor*. New York: Trident Press, 1971.

Robbins, Sidney M. and Robert B. Stobaraugh. *Money in the Multinational Enterprise*. New York: Basic Books, 1974.
This is written from a financial point of view almost exclusively and intends to help resolve financial problems encountered abroad.

Robertson, James. *Profit or People? The New Social Role*. London, England: Calder & Boyars Ltd., 1975.

Articles

Abelson, Alan. "Let It All Hang Out? Revised Standards of Disclosure May Go Too Far." *Barron's* 54 (July 1, 1974): 7+.

Acton, Harry Burrows. "Let's Be Proud of the Capitalists." (S. Smiles) *Director* 25 (July 1972): 68–70.

Aiken, Eric. "Full Disclosure? A Close Scrutiny of the 1973 Annual Reports." *Barron's* 54 (April 15, 1974): 11–12+.

Allan, Gordon G. "Games Businessmen Play." *Cost and Management* (March/April 1974).
The game of social responsibility is discussed in the context of other financial games.

Andrews, Frederick, "Agonizing Auditors: Accountants Reassess Disclosure Standards After Business Scandals." *Wall Street Journal* 185 (June 12, 1975): 1+.

Arpan, Jeffrey S. "International Differences in Disclosure Practices: Hazard for Overseas Investment." *Business Horizons* 14 (October 1971): 67–70.

Bailey, F., Jr. "Pollution, Bankers, and Farmers." *Banking* 63 (April 1971): 54+.

"The Banker and Society [panel discussion]." *Journal of Commercial Bank Lending* 54 (January 1972): 37–50.

Belkaoui, A. "Impact on the Disclosure of Pollution Control Information on the Investors: A Behavioral Field Experiment and a Market Reaction Investigation." *Journal of Finance* 29 (December 1974): 1586.

Benston, George J. "Required Disclosure and the Stock Market." *American Economic Review* 63 (March 1973): 132–155.

Bigney, B. L. "Ecology Considerations For the Trust Department." *Trusts and Estates* 113 (May 1974): 284–287+.

"A Black Bank Rides Out Money Market Storms—With Profits, Too [First Independence National Bank, Detroit, Michigan]." *Banking* 67 (March 1975): 66–67+.

Boorman, John T. "The Prospects For Minority-Owned Commercial Banks: A Comparative Performance Analysis." *Journal of Bank Research* 4 (Winter 1974): 263–279.

Brainard, W. and F. T. Dolbear. "Social Risk and Financial Markets." *American Economic Review* 61 (May 1971): 360–370+.

Briloff, Abraham J. "Full and Fair Disclosure." *Barron's* 51 (November 1, 1971): 9+.

Briloff, Abraham J. "We Often Paint Fakes." *Vanderbilt Law Review* (January 1975).
A case study on how pooling takes place with an emphasis on "dirty pooling."

Brimmer, Andrew F. "Black Banks: An Assessment of Performance and Prospects." *Journal of Finance* 26 (May 1971): 379–405+.

Brown, R. Gene. "Ethical and Other Problems in Publishing Financial Forecasts." *Financial Analysts Journal* 28 (March 1972): 38–45+.

Caroll, T. E. "Environmental Controls and Their Relation to the Financial Community." *Journal of Commercial Bank Lending* 54 (April 1972): 36–42.

Casey, William J. "Financial Disclosure, Investor Confidence, and Corporate Credibility." *Financial Executive* 40 (December 1972): 18–22.

Casey, William J. "Investor Relations and Corporate Credibility." *Wall Street Business Analyst* 129 (February 1973): 4–5+.

Casey, William J. "Responsibilities and Liabilities in Corporate Life." *Conference Board Record* 9 (February 1972): 51–54.

Casey, William J. "What Next on Disclosure?" *Commercial and Financial Chronicle* 215 (May 11, 1972): 1497+.

Cates, D. C. "Role of Financial Disclosure in Analyst Relations." *The Bankers Magazine* 155 (Winter 1972): 87–89.

Chen, R. S. "Social and Financial Stewardship." *The Accounting Review* 50 (July 1975): 533–543.

Collins, S. "New York's First Women's Bank: Is It Still A Viable Idea?" *Commercial and Financial Chronicle* 220 (February 10, 1975): 1+.

"Conflicts of Interest and Professional Inadequacies in the Securities Industry." New York Society for Ethical Culture. Center for Applied Ethics (October 1974): 19 pp. [Free—2 West 64th Street, New York, New York 10023].

"Corporations Better Get Used to Baring Their Souls in Public." *Industry Week* 170 (July 26, 1971): 18+.

Cummings, John J. "How Much Disclosure by Banks Makes Good Public Policy?" *Banking* 67 (August 1975): 38+.

Davids, L. E. "Bank Loans and the Arithmetic of the Quality of Life." *The Bankers Magazine* 155 (Spring 1972): 33–40.

DeWitt, Karen. "The Small Business Administration: Hey Buddy, Can You Spare Me a Share in the System." *Black Enterprise* 5 (January 1975): 25–27.

"Disclosure Roundup: What Should Corporations Be Required to Disclose to the Public, and Why?" *Mergers and Acquisitions* 7 (Summer 1972): 5–16.

Doctors, Samuel I. and others. "The Impact of Minority Banks on Communities." *Bankers Monthly* (Boston) 158 (Spring 1975): 84–91.

Duker, Jacob M. and T. Gregory Morton. "Black-Owned Banks: Issues and Recommendations." *California Management Review* 17 (Fall 1974): 78–85.

Edelstein, Robert H. "Improving the Selection of Credit Risks: An Analysis of a Commercial Bank Minority Lending Program." *Journal of Finance* 30 (March 1975): 37–55.

Edwards, J. B. "People Problems and Human Solutions." *Management Accounting* 56 (February 1975): 32–34.

Edwards, Robert M. "Socially Desirable Loans and Bank Regulation—A Quandary." *Journal of Commercial Bank Lending* 53 (May 1971): 12–15.

Einzig, P. "Inflation Is Unethical." *Commercial and Financial Chronicle* 217 (January 25, 1973): 336.

Friedman, J. J. and M. N. Friedman. "Relative Profitability and Monopoly Power." *Conference Board Record* 9 (December 1972): 49–58.

"Full Disclosure Due All Investors, Says SEC Chief." *Burroughs Clearing House* 56 (December 1971): 28.

Gapay, Les. "Losing Cause." *The Wall Street Journal* 180 (August 9, 1972): 1+.
Do-good mutual funds find customers rare and profits elusive indeed.

Gardner, Charles. "What a Bank Can Do in a Ghetto." *Banking* 64 (January 1972): 36–37+.
Louisiana National Bank's Eden Park Loan Office in Baton Rouge is now center of a brisk small loan business.

Gillis, John G. "Responsibilities of Professionals Under Securities Law." *Financial Analysts Journal* 30 (March 1974): 12+.

Goldberg, Charles. "Policing Responsibilities of the Securities Bar." *New York Law Forum* 19 (Fall 1973): 221–268.
A discussion of the attorney-client relationship and the code of professional responsibility–considerations for expertizing securities attorneys.

"Great Banking Retreat (Special Report)." *Business Week* (April 21, 1975): 46–102.

Green, Wayne E. "Irate Attorneys." *Wall Street Journal* 179 (February 15, 1972): 1+.
On the disclosure issue.

Goolrick, Robert M. "Some Disclosure Problems in Acquisition Proxy Statements and Prospectuses." *Business Lawyer* 28 (November 1972): 111–126.

Gudiness, Thomas J. "The Communication Problem in Pension Trust Management." *Conference Board Record* 10 (April 1973): 63–64.

Hanscombe, D. "Growth and Social Responsibility." *Banker* 124 (June 1974): 619+.

Hardwick, Leo P. "How to Size Up Requests for Charity." *Banking* 65 (June 1973): 38+.

Hardy, C. Colburn. "Enhancing Community Life. *Banking* 65 (December 1972): 17–19.
A report on various things banks are now doing.

Heyne, Paul T. "The Free-Market System Is the Best Guide for Corporate Decisions." *Financial Analysts Journal* (September/October 1971): 26–27, 72–73.

"How a Social Conscience Shapes Banking." *Business Week* (September 15, 1973): 140–141.

"How Much Should the Banks Tell Investors?" *Business Week* (November 10, 1975): 107–108.
CPA's are in the middle as bankers and regulators debate problem areas.

Hyatt, James C. "Early Warning Systems: Auditors, Outside Directors Set up Panels to Find Firms' Woes Before Crises Occur." *Wall Street Journal* 179 (May 31, 1972): 36.

"An Interview with Andrew Brimmer: A Leading Economist Talks About Black Banks, Business and Economic Development." *Black Enterprise* 3 (October 1972): 41+.

Irons, Edward D. "Black Banking—Problems and Prospects." *Journal of Finance* 26 (May 1971): 407–425+.

Kaufman, K. A. "Corporate Secrecy: Nader Finds Himself Some New Raiders." *Iron Age* 208 (November 18, 1971): 23.

Keane, Simon M. "Portfolio Theory, Corporate Objectives and the Disclosure of Accounting Data." *Accounting and Business Research* 4 (Summer 1974): 210–219.

Kell, Walter G. "The SEC's New Disclosure Rule on Forecasts." *Michigan Business Review* 25 (May 1973): 17–25.

Langton, J. F. "Corporate Responsibility and Mainstream Decisions (Bank of America)." *Trusts and Estates* 114 (July 1975): 470–473.

"Let's Blow the Whistle on the Securities Game." *American Bar Association Journal* 60 (April 1974): 461–464.

Long, J. "Wealth, Welfare, and the Price of Risk." *Journal of Finance* 27 (May 1972): 419–433+.

Loomis, P. A., Jr. "Current SEC Posture in Accounting and Financial Reporting." *Journal of Commercial Bank Lending* 57 (November 1974): 18–25.

Lurie, A. J. and V. S. Pastena. "How Promptly Do Corporations Disclose Their Problems?" *Financial Analysts Journal* 31 (September 1975): 55–61.

McConnell, Richard M. M. "Take a New Look at Women Borrowers." *Banking* 66 (August 1973): 26–28+.

McGrath, Phyllis S. "Disclosing Financial Forecasts: Is Anyone in Favor?" *Conference Board Record* 11 (January 1974): 34–36.

Marsh, James. "Viewing the Loss Experience on Minority Enterprise Loans." *The Bankers Magazine* 154 Winter 1971): 84–87.

Miller, F. R. "Environmental Investing." *Journal of Commercial Bank Lending* 53 (May 1971): 32–35.

Morthland, R. J. "Banker and the Energy Crisis." *Journal of Commercial Bank Lending* 56 (June 1974): 13–21.

Nadler, P. S. "Energy Crisis and Bank Lending Policy." *Journal of Commercial Bank Lending* 56 (March 1974): 17–22.

"The 1970 Bank Secrecy Act and the Right of Privacy." *William and Mary Law Review* 14 (Summer 1972): 929–952.
  A discussion of the act requiring financial institutions to maintain records and to submit reports of large currency transactions.

Nourallah, Fayez. "Proper Disclosure in Accounting Reports." *National Public Accountant* 17 (May 1972): 23–25.

Owens, Charles. "Justice Department Warns Banks: No Political Campaign Loans." *Banking* 63 (May 1971): 29+.

Owens, Charles. "What Is the Banker's Role in Politics?" *Banking* 64 (July 1971): 17–19+.

Pacey, Margaret D. "Slamming the Black Door? Bond Buyers Grow Uneasy over Moral Obligations." *Barron's* 54 (June 3, 1974): 5+.

Paton, William A. "Financial Misrepresentation and Mismeasurement." *Financial Executive* 41 (April 1973): 14–21.

Patterson, Pat. "Dispatches from the Banking Battlefield." *Black Enterprise* 6 (October 1975): 37+.
Recession woes fail to halt continuing growth of nation's black banks.

Perham, John C. "Those Controversial Executive Loans." *Dun's Review* (October 1974): 57–61.
The ethics of low-cost and no-cost in house loans.

Poirier, Robert D. "Financial Forecasts: To Disclose—or Not to Disclose." *Magazine of Bank Administration* 50 (March 1974): 26–31+.

Purcell, J. L. "Telling the Company's Financial Story: Some Sensitive Issues." *Conference Board Record* 11 (April 1974): 45–49.

Quantius, Frances W. "Elimination of Regulatory Inequities." *Bulletin of Business Research* (Ohio State University) 49 (September 1974): 1–3.

Roberts, Markley. "The Curtain of Conglomerate Secrecy." *American Federationist* 78 (April 1972): 20–23.

Root, A. "On Banking the Social Conscience (Chase Manhattan Capital)." *The Bankers Magazine* 155 (Winter 1972): 64–66.

Rowe, Mary P. "When the Employer Faces Day Care Decisions: Cost-Benefit Analysis and Other Decision Making Tools." *Sloan Management Review* 14 (Spring 1973): 1–11.

Rule, J. "Merchant Banks' Accounts—the Need for Disclosure." *The Banker* 122 (December 1972): 1645–1647+.

"SEC: Tell Why Auditors Are Fired." *Business Week* (October 14, 1972): 24.

"Security Analyst: How Do You Equate Conscience and Profits?" *Magazine of Wall Street* 128 (May 8, 1971): 9–11.

Seidler, Lee J. "Public Disclosure Is Not Public." *Financial Analysts Journal* 28 (July 1972): 89+.

"Selective Reporting?" *Forbes* 107 (March 15, 1971): 51+.

Shades, R. C. "Banks and Public Interest Responsibility." *The Bankers Magazine* 156 (Autumn 1973): 50–54.

Shrank, John. "Case of the Disclosure Debate." *Harvard Business Review* 50 (January 1972): 142–144+.

"Should Finance Do More than Keep Score?" *Industry Week* 174 (July 31, 1972): 24–26.

Singhyi, Surendra S. "Corporate Management's Inclination to Disclose Financial Information." *Financial Analysts Journal* 28 (July 1972): 66–73.

Smith, J. E. "Bank Supervision and the Public Interest." *Trusts and Estates* 113 (April 1974): 208–210+.

Sommer, A. A., Jr. "Expanding Role of Enforced Disclosure to Investors." *Commercial and Financial Chronicle* 213 sec 3 (May 6, 1971): 9+.

Sommer, A. A., Jr. "Random Thoughts on Disclosure as 'Consumer' Protection." *Business Lawyer* 27 (November 1971): 85–91.

Sonde, Theodore. "The Responsibility of Professionals Under the Federal Securities Laws—Some Observations." *Northwestern University Law Review* 68 (March/April 1973): 1–23.

"Sponsoring Social Change [National Conference on Bank Public Affairs]." *Burroughs Clearing House* 56 (July 1972): 22+.

Stabler, Charles and Barry Newman. "Speaking Out." *Wall Street Journal* 177 (April 28, 1971): 1.
Money managers are bucking companies on social issues.

Starr, Mike. "Cash Clash: To Fight 'Redlining.'" *Wall Street Journal* 186 (August 25, 1975): 1+.
Citizens groups turn to 'Greenlining' and depositors in poor areas use withdrawal threats to get more mortgages. "Expedience or Extortion?" The author asks.

Taft, R. W. "Disclosure: Avoiding a Roadmap to Fraud." *Public Relations Journal* 30 (April 1974): 46–53.

Talesnick, Alan L. "Corporate Silence and Rule 10b-5." *Denver Law Journal* 49 (November 3, 1973): 369–412.

Thompson, M. J. "Free Enterprise and Free Men." *Financial Executive* 42 (July 1974): 24–30.

Tietjen, A. Carl. "Financial Reporting Responsibilities." *Journal of Accountancy* 131 (January 1971): 69–73.

Tosi, Henry L., Jr. "The Human Effects of Budgeting Systems on Management." *MSU Business Topics* (Autumn 1974): 53–63.
   The budget itself and the way it is prepared and used affects managerial attitudes and behavior.

Truex, G. Robert, Jr. "Corporate Social Accountability—What Does It Mean for Banking?" *Journal of Commercial Bank Lending* 55 (October 1972): 22–29.

Wasem, G. "Cases in Conscience." *Bankers Monthly* 92 (June 1975): 22–25.

Wayman, Morris. "Towards a Technology of Social Responsibility: Problems in the Identification of Acceptable Net Benefit-Risk Ratios." *Socio-Economic Planning Science* 5 (October 1971): 483–489.

"When Consumers Laugh, Should Investors Cry?" *Financial World* 139 (February 14, 1973): 6–7.

Wright, John P. "Profitability and Social Responsibility—Are They Compatible?" *Journal of Commercial Bank Lending* 53 (May 1971): 2–11.

Marketing

Books

Allvine, Fred C. and James M. Patterson. *Highway Robbery: An Analysis of the Gasoline Crisis*. Bloomington: Indiana University Press, 1974.
   The thesis is developed that large oil companies aim to get rid of independent marketers.

Altschuler, Richard and Nicholas Regush. *IC; An Introductory Exposition of Infinite Capitalism, or the Great Nipple Plot*. 1st ed. Boston: Little, Brown, 1972.

Bailey, Earl L., ed. *Tomorrow's Marketing; A Symposium.* New York: Conference Board, 1974.
A variety of business and society issues are treated.

Berry, Leonard L. and James S. Hensel, comps. *Marketing and the Social Environment: A Readings Text.* 1st ed. New York: Petrocelli Books, 1973.

Boone, Louis E. and David L. Kurtz. *Contemporary Marketing.* Hinsdale, Illinois: Dryden Press, 1974.
A discussion of marketing ethics and social responsibilities is included.

Clewett, Robert L. and Jerry C. Olson, eds. *Social Indicators and Marketing.* American Marketing Association, 222 S. Riverside Plaza, Chicago, Illinois 60606, 1974.
Discusses social indicators and their usefulness to business and how business is responding to changing social values.

Diamond, Jay and Gerald Pintel. *Principles of Marketing.* Englewood Cliffs, New Jersey: Prentice-Hall, 1972.

Dominguez, George S. *Marketing in a Shortage Economy.* New York: AMACOM, 1974.
A hard look at the problem of allocation in the face of licit competing claims of purchasers and the broader claims of society.

Fisk, George, ed. *Marketing and Social Priorities.* American Marketing Associations, 1974.

Fisk, George. *Marketing and the Ecological Crisis.* New York: Harper & Row, 1974.

Furuhashi, Hugh Y. and E. Jerome McCarthy. *Social Issues of Marketing in the American Economy.* Columbus, Ohio: Grid, Incorporated, 1971.

Gist, Ronald R. *Cases in Marketing Management.* New York: Holt, Rinehart and Winston, Inc., 1972.

Gist, Ronald R. *Marketing and Society: A Conceptual Introduction.* New York: Holt, Rinehart and Winston, 1971.

Gist, Ronald R., ed. *Readings: Marketing and Society.* New York: Holt, Rinehart and Winston, 1971.

Goble, Ross L. and Roy T. Shaw. *Controversy and Dialogue in Marketing*. Englewood Cliffs, New Jersey: Prentice-Hall, 1975.
A collection of articles which covers a wide variety of controversial issues for marketers, including the value of marketing, consumer sovereignty, marketing ethics and social responsibility.

Hamburger, Polia Lerner. *Social Indicators: A Marketing Perspective*. Chicago: American Marketing Association, 1974.

Hartley, Robert F. *Marketing: Management and Social Change*. Scranton, Pennsylvania: Intext Educational Publishers, 1972.

Hicks, Lawrence E. *Product Labeling and the Law*. New York: AMACOM, 1974.
An AMA briefing on the law and ethics of information-giving in marketing products.

Holloway, Robert J. and Robert S. Hancock, eds. *The Environment of Marketing Management*. 3rd ed. New York: Wiley, 1974.
Societal changes and impacts are discussed.

Holloway, Robert J. and Robert S. Hancock. *Marketing in a Changing Environment*. New York: John Wiley & Sons, 1973.
Social issues are discussed.

Hustad, Thomas P. and Edgar A. Pessemier. *Will the Real Consumer-Activist Please Stand Up: An Examination of Consumers' Opinions About Marketing Practices and Their Relationships to Individual Attitudes and Behavior,* Lafayette, Indiana: Herman C. Krannert, Graduate School of Industrial Administration, Purdue University, 1972.

Kangun, Norman, ed. *Society and Marketing*. New York: Harper and Row, 1972.

Kerr, John R. and James E. Littlefield. *Marketing; An Environmental Approach*. Englewood Cliffs, New Jersey: Prentice-Hall, 1974.

Lazer, William and Eugene J. Kelley. *Social Marketing: Perspectives and Viewpoints*. Homewood, Illinois: R. D. Irwin, 1973.

Margolius, Sidney K. *The Great American Food Hoax*. New York: Walker, 1971.

Milgram, Stanley. *Obedience to Authority*. New York: Harper and Row, 1974.
Study of social irresponsibility in marketing.

Moyer, Reed, *Macro Marketing: A Social Perspective*. New York: J. Wiley and Sons, Inc., 1972.

Nicosia, Francesco. *Advertising, Management and Society: A Business Point of View*. New York: McGraw-Hill Book Company, 1974.

Nylen, David W. *Advertising: Planning, Implementation, and Control*. Cincinnati: Southwestern Publishing Company, 1975.
This attends to the role of advertising regulation in our society and evaluating consumer benefits.

Oxenfeldt, Alfred R. *Pricing Strategies*. New York: American Management Association, 1975.
The author argues that pricing decisions should be made considering objectives concerning long-term profits, growth, and social responsibility.

Sandage, C. H. and Vernon Fryburger. *Advertising Theory and Practice*. 9th ed. Homewood, Illinois: Richard D. Irwin, Incorporated, 1975.
A discussion of social effects, ethics and truth, and consumerism is included.

Sheth, Jagdish N. and Peter L. Wright, eds. *Marketing Analysis for Societal Problems*. National Conference on Social Marketing, December 1972. Urbana: University of Illinois, 1974.

Stanton, William J. *Fundamentals of Marketing*. 3rd edition. New York: McGraw-Hill, 1971.
This includes a chapter entitled "Consumerism and Marketing's Social Responsibility."

Stanton, William J. and Richard H. Buskirk. *Management of the Sales Force*. 4th ed. Homewood, Illinois: Richard D. Irwin, Incorporated, 1974.
This includes a chapter on social and ethical responsibilities of sales executives.

Webster, Frederick E. *Social Aspects of Marketing*. Englewood Cliffs, New Jersey: Prentice-Hall, Inc., 1974.

Wish, John R., ed. and Stephen H. Gamble. *Marketing and Social Issues: An Action Reader*. New York: Wiley, 1971.

Zaltman, Gerald and Philip C. Burger. *Marketing Research Fundamentals and Dynamics.* Hinsdale, Illinois: The Dryden Press, 1975. Attention is given to the issue of ethics in marketing research.

Articles

Anderson, W. Thomas and others. "Environmental Role for Marketing." *MSU Business Topics* 20 (Summer 1972): 66–72.

Anderson, W. Thomas, Jr. and William H. Cunningham. "Socially Conscious Consumer." *Journal of Marketing* 36 (July 1972): 23–31.

Barksdale, Hiram C. and William R. Darden. "Consumer Attitudes Toward Marketing and Consumerism." *Journal of Marketing* 36 (October 1972): 28–35.

Barksdale, Hiram C. and Warren A. French. "Response to Consumerism: How Change Is Perceived by Both Sides." *MSU Business Topics* (Spring 1975): 55–67.
Marketing executives and consumer advocates see the movement as call for improved performance and increased sensitivity.

Beik, Leland L. and Warren A. French. "Responsible Marketing in an Expanded Marketing Concept." *Business & Society* 14 (Spring 1974): 18–27.

Bogart, Leo. "Marketing of Public Goods." *Conference Board Record* 12 (November 1975): 20–25.

Brien, Richard H. and others. "The Challenge to Marketing Dominance: Will Social Responsibility Be Recognized?" *Business Horizons* 15 (February 1972): 23–30.

Burck, Gilbert. "High-Pressure Consumerism at the Salesman's Door." *Fortune* 86 (July 1972): 70+.

Craig, C. Samuel. "Brave New Marketing." *Business & Society* 13 (Fall 1972): 17–27.

Denenberg, Herbert S. "Those Health Insurance Booby Traps." *Progressive* 36 (September 1972): 29–33.
Misleading claims and deceptive advertising practices used in marketing certain mail order health insurance policies aimed at the elderly.

Dixon, Donald F. "Brave New Marketing Revisited." *Business & Society* 13 (Spring 1973): 10–14.
Commenting on an article by C. Samuel Craig.

El-Ansary, Adel I. "Towards a Definition of Social and Societal Marketing." *Journal of the Academy of Marketing Science* (Spring 1974): 316–321.

Farley, John U. and Harold J. Leavitt. "Marketing and Population Problems." *Journal of Marketing* 35 (July 1971): 28–33.

Feldman, Lawrence P. "Societal Adaptation: A New Challenge for Marketing." *Journal of Marketing* 35 (July 1971): 54–60.

Fisk, George. "Criteria for a Theory of Responsible Consumption." *Journal of Marketing* 37 (April 1973): 24–31.
Ecological implications of marketing decisions.

Gaedeke, Ralph. "Social Issues in Marketing Curricula." *Collegiate News and Views* (Spring 1973): 13–16.

Gelb, Betsy D. and Richard H. Brien. "Survival and Social Responsibility: Themes for Marketing Education and Management." *Journal of Marketing* 35 (April 1971): 3–9.

Greer, Thomas V. and William G. Nickels. "The Advertising Council: A Model for Social Marketing?" *Marquette Business Review* 19 (Spring 1975): 17–22.
Council's efforts in the promotion of public service advertising.

Grether, E. T. "Marketing and Public Policy: A Contemporary View." *Journal of Marketing* 38 (July 1974): 2–7.

Greyser, Stephen A. "Marketing and Responsiveness to Consumerism." *Journal of Contemporary Business* 2 (Autumn 1973): 81–94.

Gunther, Max. "But First, A Word Against Our Sponsor." *TV Guide* 20 (June 17, 1972): 6–8+; (June 24, 1972): 26–29; (July 1, 1972): 14–15+.

Hawkins, Del I. and A. Benton Cocanougher. "Student Evaluations of the Ethics of Marketing Practices: The Role of Marketing Education." *Journal of Marketing* 36 (April 1972): 61–64.

"Heating Dealer Charged with Misleading Practices." *Air Conditioning, Heating & Refrigeration News* 123 (July 19, 1971): 7.

Holton, Richard H. "Marketing Policies in Multinational Corporations." *California Management Review* 13 (Summer 1971): 57–67.

Hustad, Thomas P. and Edgar A. Pessemier. "Will the Real Consumer Activist Please Stand Up: An Examination of Consumers' Opinions About Marketing Practices." *Journal of Marketing Research* 10 (August 1973): 319–324.

"Join the Activists, Don't Fight Them, Marketers Are Advised." *Industry Week* 171 (November 1, 1971): 8–10.

Jones, J. Richard. "Needed: Socially Responsible Marketing." *Atlanta Economic Review* (July-August 1972): 30–34.

Kangun, Norman. "Environmental Problems and Marketing: Saint or Sinner?" Prepared for presentation and discussion at the *National Conference on Social Marketing, University of Illinois,* Champaign-Urbana, December 2–5, 1972.

Kangun, Norman. "Societal Issues in the Marketing Curriculum: An Optimistic Assessment." *Journal of Marketing* 37 (April 1973): 60–63.

Kassarjian, Harold H. "Incorporating Ecology into Marketing Strategy: The Case of Air Pollution." *Journal of Marketing* 35 (July 1971): 19–27.

Keane, John G. "On Professionalism in Advertising." *Journal of Advertising* (Fall 1974): 6–12.
Among criteria included in this discussion of professionalism are codes of ethics, ethics enforcement, integrity, social responsibility.

Kelley, Eugene J. "Socio-Marketing and Marketing Education." *The Southern Journal of Business* 7 (May 1972): 11–19.

King, William R. and David I. Cleland. "Environmental Information Systems for Strategic Marketing Planning." *Journal of Marketing* 38 (October 1974): 35–40.

Kinnear, Thomas C. and others. "Ecologically Concerned Consumers: Who Are They?" *Journal of Marketing* 38 (April 1974): 20–24.

Knauer, Virginia H. "Tomorrow's Marketing World." *Managerial Planning* (September/October 1971): 36–39.

Kotler, Philip. "What Consumerism Means for Marketers." *Harvard Business Review* 50 (May/June 1972): 48–57.

Kotler, Philip and Gerald Zaltman. "Social Marketing: An Approach to Planned Social Change." *Journal of Marketing* 35 (July 1971): 3–12.

Kotler, Philip and Sidney J. Levy. "Demarketing, Yes, Demarketing." *Harvard Business Review* 49 (November/December 1971): 74–80.

Landon, E. L. "The Invisible Backhand or the 'New Marketing Concept' Must Be Turning Adam Smith in His Grave." *Journal of the Academy of Marketing Science* (Fall 1973): 132–137.

"Leo Burnett on Integrity." *Marketing/Communications* 299 (December 1971): 53–55.

Loudenback, Lynn J. and John W. Goebel. "Marketing in the Age of Strict Liability." *Journal of Marketing* 38 (January 1974): 62–66.

Luck, David J. "Social Marketing: Confusion Compounded." *Journal of Marketing* 38 (October 1974): 70–72.

"Market Research Must Handle Consumerism With Kid Gloves.: *Chemical Marketing Reporter* 202 (September 18, 1972): 4+.

"Marketing: In Today's Environment, for Changing Markets, with Sharper Tools." *Wharton Quarterly* (Fall 1972): Special issue.

"Marketing's Changing Social/Environmental Role." *Journal of Marketing* 35 (July 1971): 1–72.

Martilla, John A. and Davis W. Carvey. "Four Subtle Sins in Marketing Research." *Journal of Marketing* 39 (January 1975): 8–15.

Mazze, Edward M. "Current Marketing Practice: Some Social Implication." *Marquette Business Review* (Summer 1971): 86–89.

Michman, Ronald D. "Impact of Consumerism: A Response Needed in Product Planning." *Business & Economic Dimensions* 9 (May/June 1973): 7–11.

Mueller, Robert Kirk. "ECO and the CEO: Strategic Rereat or Strategic Advance." *Industrial Marketing Management* (December 1974): 319–330.

Richie, J. R. Brent and Roger J. LaBreque. "Marketing Research and Public Policy: A Functional Perspective." *Journal of Marketing* 39 (July 1975): 12–19.

Rubin, R. S. "Franchising: A Marketing System to Improve Inner City Conditions." *Journal of the Academy of Marketing Science* (Winter 1974): 278–289.

Dr. Rubin suggests the franchise system may be able to make significant contributions to the race/poverty dilemma prevalent in today's cities.

"A Symposium on the Societal Implications of Marketing." *Journal of Consumer Affairs* 5 (Summer, 1971): 70–87.

Schwartz, George. "Marketing: The Societal Concept." *University of Washington Business Review* 31 (Autumn 1971): 31–38.

Spence, Homer E. and Reza Moinpour. "Fear Appeals in Marketing— A Social Perspective." *Journal of Marketing* 36 (July 1972): 39–43.

Sturdivant, Frederick D. and A. Benton Cocanougher. "What Are Ethical Marketing Practices?" *Harvard Business Review* 51 (November 1973): 39–43.

Takas, Andrew. "Societal Marketing: A Businessman's Perspective." *Journal of Marketing* 38 (October 1974): 2–7.

Tauber, Edward M. "How Market Research Discourages Major Innovation." *Business Horizons* 17 (June 1974): 22–26.

Tirmann, Ernst A. "Should Your Marketing Be Audited." *European Business* (Autumn 1971): 49–56.

Tittley, John T. "Global Communicators Must Meet Social, Economic, Political Pressures with Candor." *Industrial Marketing* 60 (July 1975): 67–69.

Trombetta, William L. and Timothy Wilson. "Foreseeability of Misuse and Abnormal Use of Products by the Consumer." *Journal of Marketing* 39 (July 1975): 48–55.

Tybout, Alice M. and Gerald Zaltman. "Ethics in Marketing Research: Their Practical Relevance." *Journal of Marketing Research* 11 (November 1974): 357–368.

Wilkie, William L. and David M. Gardner. "Role of Marketing Research in Public Policy Decision Making." *Journal of Marketing* 38 (January 1974): 38–47.

Wills, Gordon. "Marketing's Social Dilemma." *European Journal of Marketing* (Spring 1974): 4–14.

Yoell, W. A. "Abuse of Psychology by Marketing Men." *Marketing/Communications* 298 (August 1970): 42–44.

Production

Books

Epstein, Samuel S. and Richard D. Grundy, ed. *Consumer Health and Product Hazards—Cosmetics and Drugs, Pesticides, Food Additives.* Cambridge: MIT Press, 1974.

Epstein, Samuel S. and Richard D. Grundy, ed. *Legislation of Product Safety.* Cambridge: MIT Press, 1974.

Gray, Irwin, Albert L. Bases, Charles H. Martin, and Alexander Sternberg. *Product Liability: A Management Response.* New York: AMACOM, 1975.

Kimble, William. *Federal Consumer Product Safety Act: Including the Federal Hazardous Substances Act, the Flammable Fabrics Act, the Poison Prevention Packaging Act, the Refrigerator Safety Act.* St. Paul: West Publishing Company, 1975.

Organization for Economic Cooperation and Development. Committee on Consumer Policy. *Consumer Protection Against Toxicity of Cosmetics and Household Products: Report by the Committee on Consumer Policy.* Washington: OECD Publications center, 1974.

Peters, George A. *Product Liability and Safety.* Washington: Coiner Publications, 1971.

Rheingold, Paul D. *Product Liability, 1974.* New York: Practising Law Institute, 1974.

Scher, Irving. *Consumer Product Safety Act.* New York: Practising Law Institute, 1973.

Scher, Irving. *Developing Trends Under the Consumer Product Safety Act.* New York: Practising Law Institute, 1974.

Articles

"The Automobile Manufacturer's Liability to Pedestrians for Exterior Design: New Dimensions in 'Crashworthiness'." *Michigan Law Review* 71 (August 1973): 1654–1675.

Bacot, Eugene. "Fine Lines for Quality." *Business Administration* (October 1971): 91+.
On product safety.
Assigning responsibility for poor quality control and introducing better procedures.

"Battle Lines Drawn on Vinyl Chloride Issue." *Chemical and Engineering News* 52 (February 25, 1974): 16.
On product safety.

Bedeian, Arthur G. "Consumer Perception of Price as an Indicator of Product Quality." *MSU Business Topics* 19 (Summer 1971): 59–65.

Bennigson, Lawrence A. and Arnold I. Bennigson. "Product Liability: Manfacturers Beware!" *Harvard Business Review* (May-June 1974): 122–132.

Berenson, Conrad. "The Product Liability Revolution: Let the Manufacturer and Seller Be Sued." *Business Horizons* 15 (October 1972): 71–80.

Berenson, Conrad. "Product Liability: Viewpoints for the Purchaser." *Journal of Purchasing* 9 (May 1973): 5–11.

Brehm, H. E. "Product Safety: What Is Industry's Role?" *National Underwriter Property and Casualty Insurance Edition* 77 (October 12, 1973): 43–45+.

Burt, David N. "Understanding Quality Control." *Journal of Purchasing* 9 (May 1973): 12–24.

"Consumer Product Safety Act Seen Affecting Business Actions." *Commerce Today* 5 (June 9, 1975): 7–8.

Coop, David D. "A New Feature in the Marketing Environment: The Law of Product Liability." *Mississippi Business Review* 32 (June and July 1971): 3–6, 3–7+.

De Ment, James A., Jr. "International Products Liability: Toward A Uniform Choice of Law Rule." *Cornell International Law Journal* 5 (No. 1 1972): 75–97.

"Detroit's Liability Dilemma." *Automotive Industry* 144 (April 1, 1971): 20.

"Dow's Big Push for Product Safety." *Business Week* (April 21, 1973): 82+.

"Ecology Solution Saves $80,000: Switch to Airless Painting Eliminated Ford's Pollution Problems." *Product* (July 1975): 74.

Emerg, John T. and Clark A. Hawkins. "Sound Full Management Allows Some Social Considerations." *Arizona Review* 22 (October 1973): 1–8.

"Engineers Play Bigger Role as Lawsuits Go After Poor Design." *Industry Week* 169 (May 3, 1971): 15–16.

"A Flood of Shoddy Products—What's Being Done to Stem It." *US News and World Report* 78 (February 24, 1975): 39–40.

Gaedeke, Ralph. "Consumer Attitudes Toward Products 'Made In' Developing Countries." *Journal of Retailing* 49 (Summer 1973): 13–24.

Gray, Albert W. "Privity, Probity and Producers." *Purchasing* 70 (May 27, 1971): 25–29.
Manufacturers' ads make them liable for defective products.

Haft, Steven. "The Human Cost of Production." *Ripon Forum* 8 (July 1972): 38–41.
The emphasis is on the role of government.

Hise, Richard T. and Michael A. McGinnis. "Product Elimination: Practices, Policies, and Ethics." *Business Horizons* 18 (June 1975): 25–32.

Johnson, Michael L. "End of the Line for Weak Products?" *Industry Week* 186 (September 15, 1975): 25–29.

Karlin, E. W. "Maintaining Product Safety in a Multinational Corporation." *SAM Advanced Management Journal* 40 (Winter 1975): 22–28.

McCarthy, Colman. "The Faulty School Buses." *Saturday Review: The Society* (March 11, 1972): 50–56.
A case history on a G.M. product from Robert L. Heilbroner's book, *In the Name of Profit: Profiles in Corporate Greed.*

"Now There's a Way to Rate a Product's Environmental Cost." *Industry Week* 179 (December 17, 1973): 22+.

"Product Improvement Never Ends." *Purchasing* 70 (March 4, 1971): 57–72.

"Product Safety—Everyone's Concern." *Economic Priorities Report* 4 (No. 6, 1974): 5–20.

Reisman, G. "Myth of Planned Obsolescence." *Commercial and Financial Chronicle* 217 (June 7, 1973): 1967+.

Roberts, Dominic. "Obsolescence—or Products for Posterity?" *Business Administration* (August 1973): 20–22.
   With the consumerist cause receiving at least some government backing, companies are beginning to think twice about building obsolescence into products; but there is no simple answer to the problem.

Rukeyser, William Simon. "Fact and Foam in the Row over Phosphates."*Fortune* (January 1972): 71+.

Saunders, M. L. "An Innovative Approach to International Products Liability." *Law and Policy in International Business* 4 (No. 2, 1972): 187–219.
   This represents the work of the Hague Conference on Private International Law.

Sheridan, John H. "Are We Making 'Em' Like We Used To?" *Industry Week* 178 (July 23, 1973): 24–29.

Singer, James W. "Product Safety Efforts Challenged as Being Too Costly." *National Journal of Reports* 7 (May 3, 1975): 658–662+.

Slom, Stanley H. "Penney's Labs Reject Weak-Kneed Trousers, Other Faulty Goods; Tests Seek to Protect Firm and Serve Its Customers." *Wall Street Journal* 177 (May 13, 1971): 1+.

Smith, Thomas H. F. "Product Liability: Get It on the Record." *Management Review* 60 (January 1971): 4–10.

"Strict Liability for Defective Products in Iowa." *Iowa Law Review* 56 (February 1971): 707–715.

"Strict Standards Set for Vinyl Chloride." *Chemical and Engineering News* 52 (October 7, 1974): 5.

Thorp, Bruce E. "Senate Committee Nears Action on Bill to Create Product Safety Agency." *National Journal* 3 (September 11, 1971): 1889–1894.

Varble, Dale, "Social and Environmental Considerations in New Product Development." *Journal of Marketing* 36 (October 1972): 11–15.

Weaver, Paul H. "On the Horns of the Vinyl Chloride Dilemma." *Fortune* 90 (October 1974): 150–153+.

Worthing, P. M. "Improving Product Deletion Decision Making." *MSU Business Topics* 23 (Summer 1975): 29–38.

Public Relations

Books

Barmash, Isador. *The World Is Full of It.* New York: Delacorte Press, 1974.
    The author includes a discussion of the responsibility of public relations people in dealing with business credibility problems.

Biddlecombe, Peter, ed. *Goodwill: The Wasted Asset.* London: Business Books, 1971.

Canfield, Bertrand R. and H. Frazier Moore. *Public Relations: Principles, Cases and Problems.* Homewood, Illinois: Richard D. Irwin, Incorporated, 1973.
    A section on the evolution of public relations and corporate social responsibility is included.

Cross, Frank L. and Roger W. Ross. *Corporate Communicator's Guide for Environmental Control.* Westport, Connecticut: Technomic Publishing Company, 1973.

Cutlip, Scott M. and Allen H. Center. *Effective Public Relations.* 4th edition. Englewood Cliffs, N.J.: Prentice-Hall, 1971.
    Indicates concern for ethical issues as well as effective public relations.

Evans, Laurence. *The Communication Gap: The Ethics and Machinery of Public Relations and Information.* London: C. Knight, 1973

Gilbert, Douglas L. *Natural Resources and Public Relations.* Washington: Wildlife Society, 1971.

Henry, Kenneth. *Defenders and Shapers of the Corporate Image.* New Haven, Connecticut: College and University Press Services, Incorporated, 1972.
This includes a discussion of ethics in public relations.

Hill, John W. *The Function of Public Relations in Helping to Restore Confidence in American Institutions.* A lecture sponsored by the foundation for Public Relations Research and Education at the 16th annual Institute of the Public Relations Society of America, 1974.

Lerbinger, Otto and Nathaniel H. Sperber. *Key to the Executive Head.* Reading, Mass.: Addison-Wesley Publishing Company, 1975.
This study includes a section on social accountability.

Lesly, Philip. *The People Factor: Managing the Human Climate.* Homewood, Ill.: Dow Jones-Irwin, 1974.
This gives an analysis of the current turmoil in society.

Lloyd, Herbert M. *Standards and Ethics of Public Relations Practice.* IPRA, 1973.
Gold Paper #1 of the International Public Relations Association.

Markham, Victor W. *Planning the Corporate Reputation.* London: Allen and Unwin, 1972.

Articles

Adams, Robert T. "Is the Public's Grudge Against Business a Myth?" *Public Relations Journal* 29 (July 1973): 22–24.

Allen, Audrey. "Corporate Advertising: Its New Look." *Public Relations Journal* 27 (November 1971): 6.
Professionalism and honesty are discussed.

Belliveau, Nancy. "Credibility: How Does a Company Get It? How Does a Company Lose It?" *Institutional Investor* 7 (February 1973): 27–33.

Boyd, Robert S. "Can Public Relations Close Advertising's Credibility Gap?" *Public Relations Journal* 27 (November 1971): 34–36+.

"Business and the AAS: The New Challenge to Public Relations." *Public Relations Quarterly,* Volume 15, number 2, 1970.
The entire issue is devoted to the topic business and society issues.

Chambliss, Darden and Daniel J. Walsh. "Working with the Environmental Press." *Public Relations Journal* 29 (May 1973): 22–24.

Cheney, Richard E. "New SEC Rules Affecting PR." *Public Relations Journal* 27 (February 1971): 18–20.

Cort, Stewart S. "Speak Out for Truth." *Industry Week* 175 (November 27, 1972): 43.

"Counterattack—Business Acts to Improve a Tarnished Image; Picking Up Steam." *US News and World Report* 75 (October 8, 1973): 49–51.
  A broad campaign to upgrade industry's standing with consumers and to demolish myths about the whole US economic system is discussed.

Danko, Donald E. "A Perspective on Corporate Communications." *Public Relations Journal* 30 (August 1974): 10+.
  The author discusses the need to tell the story and maintain credibility.

Diggins, Edward P. "Put on Your Overcoat: SEC Announces Phase 1 of Disclosing Corporate Prospects." *Public Relations Journal* 28 (October 1972): 16–19.
  A discussion about the role of public relations counsel.

Dilley, Steven C. "External Reporting of Social Responsibility." *MSU Business Topics* (Autumn 1975).

Durbin, William A. "PR at the Multinational Level: Let's Not Repeat Domestic Mistakes." *Management Review* 63 (April 1974): 12–18·

"Europeans Offer Split Image of U.S. Multinationals." *Industry Week* 174 (July 17, 1972): 26–27.

Fleischer, Arthur. "The Twelve Pillars of Corporate Public Relations." *Corporate Financing* 4 (July/August 1972): 28–34.

Fuqua, J. B. "Can There Be Corporate Democracy?" *Public Relations Journal* 29 (April 1973): 10–12.
  The criteria for corporate decision making are discussed with attention to ethical justification for certain management and Board of Directors policies.

Galli, Anthony. "Corporate Advertising: More than Just a Nice Warm

Feeling All Over." *Public Relations Journal* 27 (November 1971): 19–23.

    The article argues that corporate advertising for its own sake is stupid and immoral.

Hardy, Kenneth G. "Whatever Happened to Image." *Business Quarterly* 35 (Winter 1970): 70–76.

Hill, G. Christian. "Flak for Flacks: Financial Public Relations Men Are Warned They're Liable for Their Clients' Puffery." *Wall Street Journal* 179 (March 16, 1972): 34.

Hodges, Luther, Jr. "The New Challenge for Public Relations." *Public Relations Journal* 31 (August 1975): 8–14.

    "Public erosion of confidence in capitalism has created one of our greatest opportunities and heaviest obligations," says Hodges.

"How Press Agents Handle Polluters." *Sales Management* 106 (January 15, 1971): 53.

Kehoe, Edward J. "Federal Occupational Safety and Health Act: Its Impact on Management, Safety and Public Relations." *Public Relations Journal* 28 (August 1972): 25–28.

Kinney, Richard J. "Corporate Response to Social Challenge." *Public Relations Journal* 27 (August 1971): 13–15+.

Knauer, Virginia. "And Now a Word from the Consumer." *Public Relations Journal* 28 (December 1972): 6–7+.

Lesly, Philip. "Business Faces a Change of Voice." *Public Relations Journal* 27 (November 1971): 14–16.

    Traits and skills of professional public relations will be summoned forth to help guide the revolutionary transformation of advertising in a changing environment.

Lesly, Philip. "Shifting Requirements in the Public Arena." *Public Relations Journal* 29 (December 1973): 12–13+.

Lesly, Philip. "Why the Public Isn't Listening." *Industry Week* 179 (November 19, 1973): 34–35+.

Luery, Darrell. "Keeping a Finger on the Public Pulse and the Corporate Thumb Off the Scale." *Public Relations Journal* 28 (February 1972): 14–16+.

McKee, James E., Jr. "The Public Relations Society of America Grievance Board." *Public Relations Journal* 27 (June 1971): 18–21.

Madden, Carl. "How Come Business Doesn't Explain Itself Better?" *Public Relations Journal* 28 (December 1972): 20–22+.

Nekvasil, Charles A. "Can Public Relations Do the Impossible?" *Industry Week* 176 (January 22, 1973): 26–30.

Otterbourg, Robert K. "Full Disclosure: Dream or Reality?" *Public Relations Journal* 28 (June 1972): 32–33.
Some suggestions for smaller companies faced with limitations of corporate reporting.

Paluszek, John. "Corporate Social Responsibility: PR's Last Big Chance?" *Public Relations Journal* 28 (November 1972): 66.

Pastorius, James S. "New Ecology Rules Call for PR Moves." *Public Relations Journal* 27 (June 1971): 10–11+.

"Press Is Invited to Aid Full Disclosure." *Business Week* (April 21, 1973): 28–29.

Rafe, Stephen C. "Credibility—Key to Communications Success." *Public Relations Journal* 28 (June 1972): 14–17.
Ethics in communications is discussed.

Ruckelshaus, William D. "It's Time for Environmental Truth or Consequences." *Public Relations Journal* 29 (May 1973): 6+.

Samuelson, Robert J. "The Oil Companies and the Press." *Columbia Journalism Review* 12 (January/February 1974): 13–20.
Now that the public is involved, the big firms have turned to energetic public relations. The energy debate is highlighted.

Seifert, Walter W. "Sin of Silence." *Public Relations Journal* 31 (January 1975): 11–12.
If public relations is to take its legitimate place beside the lawyer, we must establish five basic facts.

Shiefman, Saul. "Case for Action PR." *Public Relations Journal* 27 (February 1971): 22–25.

"Straight Answers Sell Business." *Industry Week* 182 (July 1, 1974): 41–42.

Thomas, Trevor. "Bridging the Credibility Gap: If Not Us, Who?" *Management Review* 63 (January 1974): 13–18.

Truitt, Richard H. "Participative Approach in Environmental Programs." *Public Relations Journal* 29 (May 1973): 31–32.

Weichmann, R. "Pollution Control: The Role of Communication in Ecology." *Management Review* 60 (April 1971): 43–45.

Weil, Andrew W. "Role of Public Relations in Environmental Action." *Public Relations Journal* 26 (November 1970): 10–12.

Wylie, Frank W. "A Common Code of Ethics." *Public Relations Journal* (February 1974): 14–15.

A discussion of a common code of ethics, with full definitions, for the press and public relations.

Purchasing

Articles

Berenson, Conrad, "Product Liability: Viewpoints for the Purchaser." *Journal of Purchasing* 9 (May 1973): 5–11.

Brookman, Denise, "Safety Has Its Purchasing Hazards." *Purchasing* 78 (February 18, 1975): 32–39.

"Business Is Good for Minority Vendors." *Purchasing* 79 (August 19, 1975): 11.

"Commercial Bribery: What You Can Do to Prevent It." *Financial Executive* 43 (November 1975): 26–30.

Concrete advice for overcoming unethical practice.

Conti, John V. "Black Is Bountiful: Firms' Buying Policies Help in the Recovery of Minority Businesses." *Wall Street Journal* 187 (January 7, 1976): 1+.

Deutsch, Claudia H. "Are Purchasing Managers Male Chauvinists." *Purchasing* 72 (February 22, 1972): 60–61.

Deutsch, Claudia H. "Minority Suppliers: No Talk, Only Action." *Purchasing* 75 (July 10, 1973): 20–21.

Deutsch, Claudia H. "Reciprocal Trade: It's Still an Issue." *Purchasing* 75 (November 6, 1973): 37+.

Reciprocity may be against the law, but that doesn't mean it's a dead issue; some purchasing managers still face pressures from customers.

Deutsch, Claudia H. "Special Report: Minority Suppliers." *Purchasing* 75 (October 16, 1973): 49–80.

Dillon, Thomas F. "Is It Safe? New Worry for Buyers." *Purchasing* 75 (November 6, 1973): 27–29.

Dillon, Thomas F. "Set Standards at the Drawing Board." *Purchasing* 72 (June 20, 1972): 53–55+.

"Don't Develop Standards—Buy Them." *Purchasing* 75 (September 4, 1973): 63–64.

Dowst, Somerby R. "Buyers Tune Up Q.C. Systems." *Purchasing* 80 (January 13, 1976): 55+.
A discussion of quality control systems and frequent complaints.

Dowst, Somerby R. "Negotiation: Use Facts—Not Fake-outs—to Get a Better Deal." *Purchasing* 79 (October 21, 1975): 47+.

Ellis, Peter R. "Special Report: Purchasing and Pollution Control." *Purchasing* 72 (April 4, 1972): 49–61.

Green, G. H. and R. D. Nordstrom. "Rewards from Being a Disloyal Buyer." *Journal of Purchasing and Materials Management* 10 (February 1974): 33–40.

Haavind, Robert C. "Are Buyers Crooks?" *Purchasing* 77 (October 8, 1974): 41.
This is a one-column opinion by the Editorial Director.

Hahn, C. K. and J. Vana. "Values, Value Systems, and Behavior of Purchasing Managers." *Journal of Purchasing* 9 (February 1973): 15–27.

Hough, Harry E. "Get the Facts Behind the Price List." *Purchasing* 70 (April 1, 1971): 35–36.
The responsibility of the purchaser and the principle of *"caveat emptor."*

Jackson, John D. "Are Your Purchasing Practices Legal?" *Purchasing* 73 (August 22, 1972): 100–102.

Jackson, John D. "Don't Accept Faulty Goods by Default." *Purchasing* 79 (July 8, 1975): 69.
Purchasers have a business and ethical obligation to get the facts.

Johnsen, Katherine. "Larger Congress Role Expected in Weapons Procurement Shifts." *Aviation Week and Space Technology* 99 (October 15, 1973): 20.
 Purchasers are advised to look at government interests.

"Minority Buying Programs Are Paying Dividends." *Purchasing* 80 (January 27, 1976): 99+.

Mullally, John J. "Your Suppliers' Energy Shortages May Be Your Problem." *Industry Week* 188 (February 2, 1976): 26-29.
 A note on how the energy crisis effects purchasers.

Owens, B. D. "The Purchasing Manager's Impact on the Environment." *Journal of Purchasing* 8 (February 1972): 58-62.
 The obligations of purchasers for the environment are explored.

"Private Purchasers Act to Increase Minority Firm Sales Nationwide." *Commerce Today* 2 (June 12, 1972): 11–14.

"Q. C. Makes Suppliers Quality-Conscious." *Purchasing* 74 (January 23, 1973): 93+.

"Quality Down? Fight Back!" *Purchasing* 76 (January 22, 1974): 63.
 Don't believe suppliers who tell you that quality standards have to be lowered in today's economy. Constant vigilance will keep shipments up to specifications.

"Quality Plummets as Sales Soar." *Purchasing* 75 (September 4, 1973): 51+.

Robertson, Jack. "Drifting Along with Watergate." *Electronic News* 18 (November 26, 1973): 20.

Shore, B. "Framework for Procurement Decisions Dominated by Environmental Constraints." *Journal of Purchasing* 8 (August 1972): 46–53.

"Should Employees Be Allowed to Accept Incentives from Suppliers?" *International Management* 30 (September 1975): 17–18.

Smith, Alton E. "Quality Control and Purchasing: A Working Partnership." *Management Review* 60 (March 1971): 22–25.

Van de Water, John. "Buy Quality, Not Just Price." *Purchasing* 70 (January 21, 1971): 45–47.

Wecksler, A. N. "Purchasing Is the Key in Plant Safety." *Purchasing* 75 (August 7, 1973). 77+.
A discussion of the role of purchasers in occupational safety.

"When the Rules Say Keep Out." *Industrial Distribution* 63 (July 1973): 59–60.

Willets, Walter E. "Affirmative Action Helps Minority Suppliers." *Purchasing* 73 (December 19, 1972): 65–58.

Woodside, Arch G., Jr. "Social Character, Purchasing New Products and Word of Mouth Advertising." *Marquette Business Review* 16 (Winter 1972): 184–191.

Research and Development

Articles

Ackoff, R. L. "Social Responsibility of Operational Research." *Operational Research Quarterly* 25 (September 1974): 361–371.

"ASCE Action on Ethical Conduct." *Civil Engineering* 44 (July 1974): 74–75.

"Battelle R&D Looks for Energy Crisis Solutions." *Industry Week* 177 (May 21, 1973): 21.

Beckman, Arnold O. "Future Problems of Research." *Research/Development* 25 (December 1974): 12–16.

Bonlden, Larry L. "Perils of Integrity." *Automation* 22 (March 1975): 42–47.

Casey, William J. "Science and Technology and World Economic Affairs." *Department of State Bulletin* 69 (November 19, 1973): 630–634.

Cole, E. N. "The New Priorities for Industrial R&D." *Research Management* 15 (January 1972): 12–18.
The President of General Motors Corporation outlines the changing role of research and urges that more attention be directed to the long term interactions of products with society and the environment.

Cordtz, Dan. "Bringing the Laboratory Down to Earth." *Fortune* 83 (January 1971): 106–108+.

"Ethics for Engineers." *Industrial Engineering* 5 (January 1973): 43–45.

Godfrey, K. A., Jr. "ASCE Tackles Land Use Planning." *Civil Engineering* 44 (July 1974): 66–69.

Guenther, George C. "OSHA: How Will It Effect Rand D?" *Research/ Development* 23 (November 1972): 24–29.

Hanson, Wesley T., Jr. and Rosmarie Van Rumker. "Multinational R & D in Practice—Two Case Studies (Eastman Kodak Corporation and Chemagro Corporation)." *Research Management* 14 (January 1971): 47–54.

Hennigan, R. D. "Economic-Explosive Ethics; Ecologic-Human Ethic." *Water and Wastes Engineering* 8 (January 1971): 24–25.

Hughson, Roy V. and Herbert Popper. "Engineering Ethics and the Environment: The Vote Is In!" *Chemical Engineering* 78 (February 22, 1971): 106–112.

"Human Biology: Ethics of Playing God." *Chemical and Engineering News* 49 (October 25, 1971): 11.

"Industrial R & D's Role in Occupational Safety and Health." *Research Management* 18 (May 1975): 8–13.

"Malpractice: Implications for Engineering Ethics." *Mechanical Engineering* 97 (October 1975): 81.

Miller, J. M. and T. H. Rockwell. "Use of Human Subjects in Human Factors Research." *Human Factors* 14 (February 1972): 35–40.

Millichamp, D. "Maintaining Ethical Standards Cuts Out Anti-Social Effects." *Engineer* 237 (July 19, 1973): 34+.

Rambo, W. R. "Who Touches the Untouchable Research?" *Research Management* 16 (May 1973): 7–11.

Rosenblueth, E. "Ethical Optimization in Engineering." *Proceedings of the American Society of Civil Engineers* 99 (April 1973): 223–243.

Rueth, Nancy. "Ethics and the Boiler Code: A Case Study." *Mechanical Engineering* 97 (June 1975): 34–36.

"Science and Ethics: A Ban on Hazardous Research." *Industrial Research* 16 (September 1974): 32+.

"Should the SAE Have Canons of Ethics?" *Automotive Engineer* 79 (April 1971): 38–39.

Turnick, T. L. "Public Versus Client Interests; An Ethical Dilemma for the Engineer." *Proceedings of the American Society of Civil Engineers* 101 (January 1975): 61–65.

Voss, Jerrold R. "Industrial Research, Social Science and Corporate Responsibility." *Research Management* 17 (September 1974): 13–16.

Business and Social Responsibility: General Works

Business and Social Responsibility: General Works

Books

Andrews, Kenneth R. *The Concept of Corporate Strategy.* Homewood, Illinois: Dow-Jones Irwin, 1971.
    An early statement in the social responsibility discussion noting that a point of coherence should be found between the company's interests and the interests of the wider society.

Anshen, Melvin, ed. *Managing the Socially Responsible Corporation.* New York: Macmillan, 1974.

Bander, Edward J., ed. *The Corporation in a Democratic Society.* Wilson, 1975.

Barnett, John, ed. *Getting Involved: A New Challenge for Corporate Activists.* New York: Dow-Jones Books, 1972.

Beeth, Gunnar. *International Management Practice: An Insider's View.* New York: American Management Associations, 1973.

Chamberlain, Neil W. *The Limits of Corporate Responsibility.* New York: Basic Books, Incorporated, 1973.
    Well-known economist and business writer describes and evaluates corporate policies in various areas of social concern. A pessimistic conclusion and truth is that we had better look elsewhere if we expect our social needs to be met. Business cannot and will not do it.

Chamberlain, Neil W. *The Place of Business in America's Future.* New York: Basic Books, 1973.
    A scholarly study of the role of business in a society of competing interests and value systems which to a large extent are shaped by business.

Committee for Economic Development (CED). *Social Responsibilities of Business Corporations*. New York: CED, 1971.
> An affirmation of the social responsibility doctrine. It is in the "enlightened self-interest" of corporations to promote the public welfare in a positive way.

Dexter, Lewis Anthony. *American Business and Public Policy*. 2nd edition. New York: Atherton Press, 1972.

Elkins, Arthur and Dennis Callaghan. *A Managerial Odyssey: Problems in Business and Its Environment*. Addison-Wesley, 1975.
> A good collection of articles and cases on most of the wide socio-ethical issues.

Evans, William D. and Robert A. Wagley. *Business and Society: 74–75*. Morristown, New Jersey: General Learning Press, 1974.
> The authors recommend this anthology for classroom use having carefully evaluated student responses after classroom exposure.

Farmer, Richard N. and W. Dickerson Hogue. *Corporate Social Responsibility.* Chicago, Illinois: Science Research Associates (259 East Erie Street), 1973.
> Focuses on the roles and obligations of the large firm in the wider society.

Fremont-Smith, Marion R. *Philanthropy and the Business Corporation*. New York: Russell Sage Foundation, 1972.
> One of the first responses of organizational management to the recognition of relevant publics and their impact is philanthropy.

Fuchs, Victor R. *Who Shall Live? Health, Economics, and Social Choice*. New York: Basic Books, 1974.
> A well researched analysis of health and medical care problems from the perspective of an economist.

Gailbraith, John Kenneth. *Economics and the Public Purpose*. Boston: Houghton Mifflin Company, 1973.

Getting Involved: A New Challenge for Corporate Activists (Wall Street Journal, eds.). New York: Dow-Jones, 1972.

Goldston, Eli. *The Quantification of Concern*. Pittsburgh: Carnegie-Mellon University, 1971.
> A moderate position on the social responsibility doctrine.

80

Greenwood, William T. *Issues in Business and Society.* 2nd Edition. Boston: Houghton Mifflin, 1971.

Jacoby, Neil H. *Corporate Power and Social Responsibility.* New York: MacMillan Publishing Compnay, 1973.

Johnson, Harold L. *Business and Contemporary Society: Framework and Issues.* Belmont, California: Wadsworth Publishing Company, 1971.

Linowes, David. *The Corporate Conscience.* New York: Hawthorne Books, 1974.
The business corporation is caught in the grips of a socio-economic revolution. One response, according to the author, is the assumption of social responsibility.

Lonstreth, Bevis and H. David Rosenbloom. *Corporate Social Responsibility & the Institutional Factor: A Report to the Ford Foundation.* New York: Praeger, 1973.
Special studies series.

Luthans, Fred and R. Hodgets. *Readings on the Current Social Issues in Business.* New York: MacMillan, 1972.

Manne, Henry G. and Henry C. Wallich. *The Modern Corporation and Social Responsibility.* Washington, D.C.: American Enterprise Institute, 1972.
A conservative view. The authors condemn notions of aggressive social responsibility actions on the part of business.

Moss, Frank E. *Initiatives in Corporate Responsibility.* Washington, D.C.: U. S. Government Printing Office, 1973.

Nader, Ralph, ed. *The Consumer and Corporate Accountability.* New York: Harcourt Brace Jovanovich, 1973.
A large selection of cases and examples of corporate irresponsibility are included here with Nader type interpretations and responses.

Newman, William. *Strategy, Policy and Central Management.* Cincinnati, Ohio: South-Western, 1971.

Paluszek, John. *Organizing for Corporate Social Responsibility.* Special study 51, New York: Presidents' Association, Inc., American Management Association, 1973.

81

Preston, Lee E. and James E. Post. *Private Management and Public Policy: The Principle of Public Responsibility.* Englewood Cliffs, N.J.: Prentice-Hall, 1975.

A sophisticated well researched volume doing justice to both the internal dynamics of corporate life and the external relationships.

Progress in the Areas of Public Concern. Milford, Michigan: General Motors Corporation, 1971.

Reiss, Alvin H. *Culture and Company.* New York: Twayne Publishing Company, 1972.

Research and Policy Committee, Committee for Economic Development. *Social Responsibilities of Business Corporations.* New York: Committee for Economic Development, 1972.

Sethi, Prakash S. *The Unstable Ground: Corporate Social Policy in a Dynamic Society.* Los Angeles: Melville Publishing Company, 1974.

Shenfield, Barbara. *Company Boards: Their Responsibilities to Shareholders, Employees, and the Community.* Mystic, Connecticut: Verry, 1971.

Social Responsibilities of Business Corporations by the Research and Policy Committee. Committee for Economic Development. New York: 1971.

Steiner, George A. *Business and Society.* New York: Random House, 1971.

Steiner, George A. *Issues in Business and Society.* New York: Random House, 1973.

Steiner, George A., ed. *Selected Major Issues in Business Role in Modern Society.* Los Angeles: Graduate School of Management, UCLA, 1973.

Watson, John H. III. *Biennial Survey of Company Contributions.* New York: The Conference Board, 1972.

Wilcox, Clair. *Public Policy Towards Business.* 4th edition. Homewood, Illinois: Richard D. Irwin, 1971.

Articles

Adam, John, Jr. "Put Profit in Its Place." *Harvard Business Review* 51 (March-April): 150–160.

Adizes, I. and J. F. Weston. "Comparative Models of Social Responsibility." *Academy of Management Journal* 16 (March 1973): 112–128.

Ahfeld, W. J. "Pragmatic Limits on Business Involvement." *Public Relations Journal* 27 (May 1971): 6–9.

Aldag, Ramon J. and Donald W. Jackson, Jr. "A Managerial Framework for Social Decision Making." *MSU Business Topics* 23 (Spring 1975): 33–40.

Alexander, Tom. "The Social Engineers Retreat Under Fire." *Fortune* (October 1972): 132+.

"Analysts Weigh Significance of Corporate Social Responsibility." *Trusts and Estates* 110 (September 1971): 756–757+.

Andrews, Kenneth R. "Can the Best Corporations Be Made Moral?" *Harvard Business Review* 51 (May-June 1973): 57–64.
The issues of the social responsibility debate are sorted out along with a normative statement favoring increased social responsibility.

Andrews, Kenneth R. "Public Responsibility in the Private Corporation." *Journal of Industrial Economics* 20 (April 1972): 135–145.
The firm has a responsibility to consider its impact on the various publics of its host environment.

Armstrong, Robert W. "Why Management Won't Talk." *Public Relations Journal* (November 1970): 6–8.

Ash, Roy L. "Realities vs. Rhetoric: The Dilemma of Social Cost." *Conference Board Record* 8 (July 1971): 38–40.

Baker, Henry G., Sr. "Identity and Social Responsibility Policies: Six Large Corporations Examined." *Business Horizons* 16 (April 1973): 23–28.

Banks, L. "Mission of Our Business Society." *Harvard Business Review* 53 (May 1975): 57–65.

Barker, R. F. "Are Profits and Social Concern Incompatible." *Pittsburgh Business Review* 41 (August/September 1971): 1–6.

Bartimole, Roldo. "Keeping the Lid On: Corporate Responsibility in Cleveland." *Business and Society Review/Innovation* 5 (Spring 1973) 96–103.

Bender, Marilyn. "Van Heusen's Hair Shirt." *New York Times* (June 4, 1972): Financial Section.
    An illuminating article on social responsibility.

Beré, J. F. "On the Mutuality of Our Interests." *Conference Board Record* 11 (July 1974): 48–50.

Beresford, Dennis, comp. "A Special Study of Social Measurement Disclosures in Annual Reports." Ernst & Ernst, 1974.

Bernstein, Jack. "Social Responsibility—Business in a Bind." *Public Relations Journal* 29 (August 1973): 14–16.
    Views of the social responsibility of business have become polarized. Some reasons why are given here.

Black, E. M. "Social Welfare Challenge for Business and Labor." *Harvard Business Review* 51 (July 1973): 6–7.

Blumberg, Phillip I. "The Politicalization of the Corporation." *The Business Lawyer* (July 1971): 1551–1587.

Blumberg, Phillip I. "Selected Materials on Corporate Social Responsibility." *Business Lawyer* (July 1972): 1275–1299.

Bradshaw, T. F. "Corporate Social Reform: An Executive's Viewpoint." *California Management Review* 15 (No. 4, 1973): 85–89.

Bradshaw, T. F. "Corporation Executive's View of Social Responsibility." *Financial Analysts Journal* 27 (September 1971): 30–31+.

Brown, Andrew M. "The Social Responsibility of Industry and Commerce." *Economic Activity* (Western Australia) 13 (July 1970): 37–39.

Browne, M. Neil and Paul F. Haas. "Social Responsibility and Market Performance." *MSU Business Topics* 19 (Autumn 1971): 7–10.

Browne, M. Neil and Paul F. Haas. "Social Responsibility: The Uncertain Hypothesis." *MSU Business Topics* 22 (Summer 1974): 47–51.

Buehler, M. and Y. K. Shetty. "Motivations for Corporate Social Action." *Academy of Management Journal* 17 (December 1974): 767–771.

Burck, Gilbert. "The Hazards of 'Corporate Responsibility'." *Fortune* 87 (June 1973): 114–117+.

"Business Fights the Social Ills in a Recession." *Business Week* (March 6, 1971): 51–54+.

"Business Goes After Urban Renewal with Profit in Mind." *Industry Week* 170 (July 12, 1971): 9–11.

Carroll, Archie B. "Corporate Social Responsibility: Its Managerial Impact and Implications." *Journal of Business Research* 2 (January 1974): 75–88.

Carroll, Archie B. "Social Responsibility and Management." *The Personnel Administrator* 20 (April 1975): 46–50.
    The theme is struck by a quote from Louis Lundborg, past chairman of the board of Bank of America: "The real question in regard to social involvement is not 'whether' but 'how much'."

Cartun, W. P. "Fact and Fiction of Social Responsibility." *SAM Advanced Management Journal* 38 (January 1973): 34–37.

Casey, William J. "Responsibilities and Liabilities in Corporate Life." *Conference Board Record* 9 (February 4, 1972): 51–54.

Cassell, Frank H. "The Social Cost of Doing Business." *MSU Business Topics* 22 (Autumn 1974): 19–26.

Challen, Peter. "Corporate Planning for Social Responsibility." *Long Range Planning* 7 (June 1974): 38–44.

"Chemical Profits Seen in Meeting Social Needs." *Chemical Marketing Reporter* 201 (March 20, 1972): 4+.

Cohn, Jules. "The New Business of Business." *Urban Affairs Quarterly* 6 (September 1970): 71–87.

"Consultant Talks Profits in Selling Social Responsibility." *Industry Week* 170 (August 30, 1971): 14+.

"Consultant Urges Business Tack to Save Our Social Institutions." *Industry Week* 172 (March 20, 1972): 15–16.

"Consumer: Will American Business Turn Social Worker?" *Magazine of Wall Street* 128 (September 13, 1971): 39.

"Corporate Good Citizenship Pays Off in Central America (United Brands)." *Industry Week* 182 (July 22, 1974): 20–21.

"Corporate Responsibility and the Problems of the City." *Journal of Contemporary Business* 3 (Spring 1974): 1–109.

"Corporation and Its Obligation." *Harvard Business Review* 53 (May 1975): 127–138.

> An interview with Xerox's C. P. McColough where this enlightened CEO makes a case for social responsibility.

Cramer, Joe J. "Acceptance of Social Responsibility and Delivery by Business." A paper presented at the American Association of Collegiate Schools of Business Assembly, (May 5, 1972).

Davenport, Maurice R. "The Alcohol Industry: Dragging Its Heels or Downright Social?" *Engage* 4 (August 1972): 37–43.

> The author calls on the alcohol industry to recognize its social responsibility in face of increasing alcoholism in U.S. . . . Industry must get involved in problems caused by its product.

Davis, Keith. "Case For and Against Business Assumption of Social Responsibilities." *Academy of Management Journal* 16 (June 1973): 312–322.

Davis, Keith. "Five Propositions for Social Responsibility." *Business Horizons* 18 (June 1975): 19–24.

> After twenty years of controversy, some support is developing for guides to the conduct of business.

Davis, Keith. "Social Involvement by Business." *University of Washington Business Review* 30 (Spring 1971): 5–13.

> An assessment of the predictable risks and benefits.

Dierkes, M. and Robert Coopock. "Corporate Responsibility Does Not Depend on Public Pressure." *Business and Society Review* (Summer 1973): 82–89.

"The Dilemma of Corporate Responsibility and Maximum Profits: An Interview with David Rockefeller." *Business and Society Review/ Innovation* (Spring 1974): 4–11.

Director, Steven M. and Samuel I. Doctors. "Do Business School Students Really Care About Social Responsibility?" *Business and Society Review/Innovation* (Spring 1973): 91–95.

"Doing Good Works on Company Time." *Business Week* (May 13, 1972): 166–168.

> Three IBM men are examples of a growing trend to give leaves for public service.

Dorsey, B. R. "Business Responsibility to Society." *Atlanta Economic Review*. 20 (October 1970): 8–13.

Drotning, Phillip. "Why Nobody Takes Corporate Social Responsibility Seriously." *Business and Society Review* 6 (Autumn 1972): 68–72.

Drucker, Peter F. and Edward K. Hamilton. "A Debate—Can the Businessman Meet Our Social Needs?" *Saturday Review of the Society* 1 (March 17, 1973): 41–53.
A debate and the rejoinders between one who says no and one who says yes to the question.

Eilbirt, Henry and I. Robert Parket. "The Corporate Responsibility Officer: A New Position on the Organization Chart." *Business Horizons* 16 (February 1973): 45–54.

Eilbirt, Henry and I. Robert Parket. "The Current Status of Corporate Social Responsibility." *Business Horizons* 16 (August 1973): 5–14.

Feldberg, Meyer. "Defining Social Responsibility." *Long Range Planning* 7 (August 1974): 39–44.

Fenn, Dan H., Jr. "Executives as Community Volunteers." *Harvard Business Review* 49 (March/April 1971): 4–16; 156-157.
The author argues that poor communication between companies, managers, and community groups undercuts the usefulness of businessmen.

"Firms Stress Public Affairs, Not Fund Raising." *Industry Week* 181 (June 24, 1974): 20+.

"Four Case Studies on What Makes a Businessman a Public Servant."
1) Pyhias, P.J., "The Profit Motive."
2) Moskowitz, Milton, "Response to Social Pressure."
3) Detman, Art, "The Lure of Subsidy."
4) Blaustein, Arthur, "The Possibilities of Partnership."
Saturday Review of the Society 1 (March 17, 1973): 54–59.

Friedman, Milton. "Economic Myths and Public Opinion." *The Alternative: An American Spectator* 9 (January 1976): 5–9.
A ringing endorsement of the free enterprise system by way of historical analysis.

Gaskill, W. J. "What's Ahead for Corporating in Social Responsibility?" *Financial Executive* 39 (July 1971): 10–16+.

Goodell, George S. "Social Responsibility and the Profit Motive." *Business & Society* 13 (Fall 1972): 17–27.

Gordon, Theodore J., Dennis L. Little, Harold L. Strudler, Donna D. Lustgarten. "A Forecast of the Interaction Between Business and Society in the Next Five Years." *Institute for the Future* Middletown, Connecticut, April 1971, Report R-21.

Gray, D. H. "Standards of Corporate Responsibility Are Changing." *Financial Analysts Journal* 27 (September 1971): 28–29+.

Griffin, Clare E. "Locus of Social Responsibility in the Large Corporation." *Michigan Business Review* 23 (March 1971): 5–10.

Gunness, Robert. "Social Responsibility: The Art of the Possible." *Business and Society Review* (Winter 1974-75): 94–99.
According to the author, the new definition of social responsibility will be couched more in human and environmental terms, less in terms of economics, technology and gross production of goods and services.

Hanrahan, George D. "Why Social Programs Fail." *Economic and Business Bulletin* (Spring-Summer 1972): 51–59.

Hanscombe, D. "Growth and Social Responsibility." *Banker* 124 (June 1974): 619+.

Hay, R. and E. Gray. "Social Responsibilities of Business Managers." *Academy of Management Journal* 17 (March 1974): 135–143.

Heckman, Jerome H. "The New Pressure for Associations to Act in the Public Interest." *Association Management* 27 (Fall 1975): 28–31.

Hill, R. "Should Firms Try to Solve Social Problems?" *International Management* 27 (April 1972): 50–51+.

Hodges, Luther H., Jr. and Milton Friedman. "Does Business Have a Social Responsibility?" *Magazine of Bank Administration* 47 (April 1971): 12+, 13–16.
Opposing sides of the social responsibility issue presented.

Hollister, Spencer. "The Dangers of Social Responsibility—Another Perspective." *The Conference Board Record* (November 1972): 54–57.

"How Business Tackles Social Problems." *Business Week* (May 20, 1972): 95–97+.

"How Social Responsibility Became Institutionalized: A Rundown of Corporate Social Action." *Business Week* (June 30, 1973): 74–79+.

Jamieson, J. K. "The Social Responsibility of the Corporation." *Lamp* 53 (Winter 1971): 1–3.

Jessup, John K. and Irving Kristol. "On Capitalism and the 'Free Society.'" *Public Interest* (Winter 1971): 101–105.

Kahn, Robert. "What Should a Good Annual Report Cover." *Business and Society Review* 14 (Summer 1975): 50–54.

Kandel, William L. "The Social Conscience in Hard Times." *Business and Society Review/Innovation* (Winter 1973/1974): 17–20.

Kappel, F. R. "Management's Responsibility to Society." *Personnel Administration* 34 (July 1971): 18–20.

Kinard, Jerry L. "About This Business of Social Responsibility." *Personnel Journal* 53 (November 1974): 825–828.
    An assessment of different views concerning social responsibility and a positive appraisal of the new doctrine.

Kriss, Ronald P. "Who Is to Do Society's Work?" *Saturday Review of the Society* 1 (March 17, 1973): 28.
    An editorial discussing industry's as opposed to government's contributions to social services.

Krum, James R. "Perspectives on the Consequences of Big Business." *MSU Business Topics* 23 (Summer 1975): 60–68.
    The basic query: can justice be achieved when the self-interest of the corporation is pitted against the public interest?

Lipson, Harry A. "Do Corporate Executives Plan for Social Responsibility?" *Business and Society Review* 12 (Winter 1974-75): 80–81.
    Yes, social goals are becoming standard in corporate planning. Statistics are given.

Loveland, John and Arthur Wahtley. "The Threat of Social Responsibility." *Business and Society* 13 (Spring 1973): 15–20.

Lundborg, Louis B. "The Lessons of Isle Vista." *The Business Lawyer* (January 1971).
    The chairman of the board, Bank of America talks about the necessity of business coming to terms with demands for business social responsibility.

89

Lundborg, Louis. "Who Says Society Is Not Our Business?" *Trusts and Estates* 110 (September 1971): 748–751.
An enlightened CEO speaks his mind.

McAlmon, George "The Corporate Boardroom: A Closed Circle." *Business and Society Review* 12 (Winter 1974-75): 64–71.
The author thinks that those outside the corporate power elite cannot influence corporate policy.

McCall, David B. "Profit: Spur for Solving Social Ills." *Harvard Business Review* 51 (May-June 1973): 46–56.

McSwiney, J. W. "Social Responsibility in Management." *American Paper Industry* 54 (August 1972): 18–19.

Manne, Henry G. "Who's Responsible? What the Anti-Corporate Zealots Are Pushing Is Coercion." *Barron's* 51 (May 17, 1971): 1+.

Mazis, Michael and Robert Green. "Implementing Social Responsibility." *MSU Business Topics* 19 (Winter 1971): 68–76.

Meyer, Randall. "The Role of Big Business in Achieving National Goals." *The Presidents Lecture Series, Florida State University,* November 26, 1974. (Available-Free Public Affairs Department, Exxon Company, Box 2180, Houston, Texas).

Michaelis, M. "Humane Technology for Business Betterment." *Conference Board Record* 10 (February 1973): 56–60.

Miljus, Robert C. "Two Views of Business Social Responsiveness: Voluntarism vs. Sociotechnical Reform." *Bulletin of Business Research* 49 (December 1974): 1–2+.

"Milton Friedman Responds." *Business and Society Review* 1 (Spring 1972): 5–16.

Monsen, R. Joseph. "Social Responsibility and the Corporation." *Journal of Economic Issues* 6 (March 1972): 125–141.
Alternatives for the future of capitalism.

Moskowitz, Milton. "Profiles in Corporate Responsibility: The Ten Worst; the Ten Best." *Business and Society Review* (Spring 1975): 28–42.

"The Movement for Corporate Responsibility." *Economic Priorities Report* 2 (April/May 1971): 1+.

Murphy, Thomas A. "The Worldwide Corporations Role in Society." *Atlanta Economic Review* 25 (January/February 1975): 38–40.

"New Role Seen for Industry in Solving U.S. Social Ills." *Industry Week* 168 (February 22, 1971): 20–21.

Parket, I. Robert and Henry Eilbirt. "The Practice of Business Social Responsibility: The Underlying Factors." *Business Horizons* 18 (August 1975): 5–10.

Parkinson, G. "Can Management Techniques Solve Social Problems?" *International Management* 26 (March 1971): 34–35+.

Preston, Lee J. "Corporation and Society: The Search for a Paradigm." *Journal of Economic Literature* 13 (June 1975): 434–463.

Preston, Paul. "The Future of Business: A Process Model of Social Responsibility." *Arkansas Business and Economic Review* 5 (August 1972): 5–10.

Raymond, Robert S. and Elizabeth Richards. "Social Indicators and Business Decisions." *MSU Business Topics* 19 (Autumn 1971): 42–46.
    With the current emphasis on environmental and human problems, new measures of society's progress need to be developed.

Richman, Barry. "Corporate Social Responsibility and Enlightened Management." *Business Quarterly* 38 (Spring 1973): 43–53.

Richman, Barry. "New Paths to Corporate Social Responsibility." *California Management Review* 15 (Spring 1973): 20–36.

Roberts, John. "DuPont in Wilmington." *Better Living* 25 (Spring 1971): 2–13.
    City's biggest ctiizen takes on a larger social role to deal with growing urban plight.

Rockefeller, David. "Corporate Task for 70's Social Action, Not Words." *Commercial and Financial Chronicle* 215 (January 6, 1972): 69.

Rockefeller, Rodman C. "Turn Public Problems to Private Account." *Harvard Business Review* 49 (January 1971): 131–138.
    Business entrepreneurs must find ways to make corporate objectives more relevant to society's major concerns. The author describes the efforts of International Basic Economy Corporation in helping to solve community and social problems in the US and abroad.

91

Rogers, T. G. P. "Partnership with Society: The Social Responsibility of Business." *Management Decision* 10 (Summer 1972): 135–142.

Schwartz, Kenneth. "How Social Activists See Business." *Business and Society Review* 14 (Summer 1975): 70–73.
    An assessment of the impact on society of social activists. The evidence shows that the public's attitudes toward business parallel the activists to have a considerable impact.

Sesser, Stanford N. "Changing Times." *The Wall Street Journal* 178 (November 2, 1971): 1+.
    An articulation of the trade-offs between economic well being and environmental well being.

Sethi, Narendra K. and Manoj K. Bhaumik. "Changing Dimensions of Corporate Social Responsibility." *Management in Government* 5 (January-March): 295–307.

Sethi, S. Prakash. "Dimensions of Corporate Social Performance: An Analytical Framework." *California Management Review* 17 (Spring 1975): 58–64.

Shocker, Alan D. and Prakash Sethi. "An Approach to Incorporating Societal Preferences in Developing Corporate Action Strategies." *California Management Review* 15 (Winter 1973): 99+.

Smith, Robert Rutherford. "Social Responsibility: A Term We Can Do Without." *Business and Society Review/Innovation* 9 (Spring 1974): 51–55.

"Social Action Survives If It's Good Business." *Industry Week* 169 (June 14, 1971): 49+.

"Social Responsibility of Business." *Journal of Contemporary Business* 2 (Winter 1973): 1–16.

"Social Responsibility Reporting." *CPA Journal* 44 (December 1974): 71–72.

Spencer, Hollister. "The Dangers of Social Responsibility—Another Perspective." *The Conference Board Record* (November 1972): 54–57.

Spitzer, Carl and Patrick Manning. "The Nuts and Bolts of Corporate Responsibility." *Business and Society Review/Innovation* (Summer 1974): 78–80.

Stabler, Charles N. "For Many Corporations, Social Responsibiilty Is Now a Major Concern." *Wall Street Journal* (October 26, 1971).

Stair, Roger. "Power and the People—the Case of Con Edison." *The Public Interest* 26 (Winter 1972): 75–99.
    Concerning the complex, interdependent relationship between consolidated Edison and New York City.

Steiner, Goerge A. "Intstitutionalizing Corporate Social Decisions." *Business Horizons* 18 (December 1975): 12–18.

Steiner, George A. "Social Policies for Business." *California Management Review* 15 (Winter 1972): 17–24.

Stephenson, Lee. "Prying Open Corporations: Tighter than Clams." ment for Corporate Responsibility." *Economic Priorities Report* 3 (March/April 1972): 1+.

Stephenson, Lee. "Prying Open Corporations: Tigher than Clams." *Business and Society Review/Innovations* (Winter 1973/1974): 43–49.

Stover, Carl F. "The Corporation and the Public Good." *Conference Board Record* 7 (December 1970): 33–36.

Tyler, Gus. "The Limits of Corporate Responsibility." *Montclair Journal of Social Sciences and Humanities* 2 (Summer 1973): 18–34.

Vanderwicken, Peter. "G.M.: The Price of Being 'Responsible.' " *Fortune* (January 1972): 99.

Voss, J. R. "Industrial Research, Social Science and Corporate Responsibility." *Research Management* 17 (September 1974): 13–16.

Votaw, Dow. "Genius Becomes Rare: A Comment on the Doctrine of Social Responsibility." Part I. *California Management Review* 15 (Winter 1972): 25–31.

Votaw, Dow. "Genius Becomes Rare: A Comment on the Doctrine of Social Responsibility." Part II. *California Management Review* 15 Spring 1973): 5–19.

Ways, Max. "Don't We Know Enough to Make Better Public Policies." *Fortune* (April 1971): 64.

Webster, B. "Company's Role in Society." *Personnel Management* 5 (November 1973): 39–41+.

Weidenbaum, M. L. "Social Responsibility Is Closer than You Think." *Michigan Business Review* 25 (July 1973): 32–35.

"Which Demands Do You Face First?" *Industry Week* 172 (January 10, 1972): 43–46.

Wileman, David. "Transferring Space-Age Management Technology." *Conference Board Record* 7 (October 1970): 50-55.

Wilson, Ian H. "Reforming the Strategic Planning Process: (Integration of Social Responsibility and Business Needs)." *Long Range Planning* 7 (October 1974): 2–6.

Winter, E. L. "Management's Role in Fixing up America." *SAM Management Journal* 39 (October 1974): 4–8.

"Xerox Gives Staff Paid Time for Social Welfare Work." *Management Advisor* 8 (November 1971): 14–15.

Business and Social Responsibility: Particular Issues

Business and Social Responsibility: Particular Issues

Changing Business and Society: New Realities

Books

Bagley, Edward R. *Beyond the Conglomerates: The Impact of the Supercorporations on the Future of Life and Business.* New York: AMACOM; American Management Associations, 1974.

Bell, Daniel. *The Coming of Post-Industrial Society.* New York: Basic Books, 1973.

Bell, Daniel. *The Cultural Contradictions of Capitalism.* New York: Basic Books, 1976.
   The author contrasts the new emerging "self-gratification ethic" with the old "protestant ethic." Capitalism is viewed ironically as being a main source of the erosion of the old ethic.

Blair, John. *Economic Concentration.* New York: Barcourt Brace Jovanovich, 1972.

Capitman, William G. *Panic in the Boardroom: New Social Realities Shake Old Corporate Structures.* Garden City, New York: Doubleday, 1973.

Cavanaugh, Gerald F. *American Business Values in Transition.* Englewood Cliffs, N.J.: Prentice-Hall, 1976.

Chamberlain, Neil W. *The Place of Business in America's Future: A Study in Social Values.* New York: Basic Books, 1973.

Conner, Patrick E. *Dimensions in Modern Management.* Boston: Houghton Mifflin Company, 1974.
   An anthology developed around management as a distinct and new institution in our social history. Changes in the ethics and ethos of corporations are treated extensively.

Corson, John J. *Business in the Humane Society*. New York: McGraw-Hill, 1971.

The impact on business of a society of changing values is the central concern of this scholarly volume.

Haas, John J. *Corporate Social Responsibilities in a Changing Society*. Brooklyn, New York: Theodore Gaus' Sons, Incorporated, 1973.

Hacker, Andrew. *The Corporation Takeover*. New York: Harper & Row, 1974.

Hamilton, Walter A. *The Negotiating Society*. Austin: Bureau of Business Research, University of Texas, 1973.

Effect of strong currents of social evolution on the relationship of business and society and the services which the Conference Board renders.

Hargreaves, John and Jan Dauman. *Business Survival and Social Change*. New York: Halsted Press, 1975.

Hickel, Walter J. *Who Owns America?* Englewood Cliffs, N.J.: Prentice-Hall, 1971.

Kienast, Philip and Douglas MacLachlan, Homer Spence, Kirk Hart. *A Study of Citizen Trust and Confidence in American Institutions*. Seattle, Washington: Graduate School of Business, University of Washington, 1974.

This research monograph is a thoroughly documented, well conceptualized study including a thoughtful evaluation of the findings. (136 pages).

Levitt, Theodore. *The Third Sector: New Tactics for a Responsive Society*. American Management Association, New York, 1974.

The author looks at the consequences of activist violence and fault finding and proposes solutions.

Mintz, Morton and Jerry S. Cohen. *AMERICA, Inc.* New York: Dial Press, Incorporated, 1971.

Monsen, Joseph. *Business and the Changing Environment*. New York: McGraw-Hill, 1973.

Major issues of consumerism, minorities, ecology are discussed along with sections on the history of business and changing American value.

Nader, Ralph and Donald Ross. *Action for Change: A Students' Manual for Public Interest Organizing.* New York: Grossman Publications, 1971.

Nader, Ralph and Mark J. Green. *Corporate Power in America.* New York: Grossman Publications, 1973.

Neubeck, Kenneth J. *Corporate Response to Urban Crisis.* Lexington, Massachusetts: D. C. Heath and Company, 1974.

Orren, Karen. *Corporate Power and Social Change: The Politics of the Life Insurance Industry.* Washington, D.C.: Johns Hopkins University Press, 1974.

Rockefeller, John D., 3rd. *The Second American Revolution: Some Personal Observations.* New York: Harper & Row, 1973.

Roeber, Richard J. C. *The Organization in a Changing Environment.* Reading, Massachusetts: Addison-Wesley, 1973.

Sethi, S. Prakash, ed. *The Unstable Ground: Corporate Social Policy in a Dynamic Society.* Los Angeles: Melville Publishing Company, 1974.

Sperber, Nathaniel. *Key to the Executive Head.* Reading, Massachusetts: Addison-Wesley, 1975.

Tarnowieski, Dale. *The Changing Success Ethic.* New York: AMA (135 West 50th Street), 1973.
A 52 page survey of responses from business executives indicating changes in the protestant ethic.

Tomeski, Edward A. and Harold Lazarus. *People Oriented Computer Systems.* New York: Van Nostrand Reinhold Company, 1975.
Advocating humane and ethical uses of computers.

Votaw, Dow and S. Prakash Sethi. *The Corporate Dilemma: Traditional Values Versus Contemporary Problems.* Englewood Cliffs, N.J.: 1973.

An in depth analysis of problems posed by the clash between traditional business values and current societal values.

Walton, Clarence G., ed. *Business and Social Progress.* New York: Praeger, 1971.

Weisskopf, Walter A. *Alienation and Economics.* New York: E.P. Dutton, 1971.

A profound reflection on the current malaise in society and the corporate dilemma.

White House Conference on the Industrial World Ahead. *A Look At Business in 1990*. Washington, D.C.: U.S. Government Printing Office, 1972.

Wortman, Max S. Jr. and Fred Luthans, eds. *Emerging Concepts in Management*.
Changing management theory and practice are described and prescribed in the light of new social realities and pressure to change and behave.

Zaltman, Gerald and Philip Kotler, Ira Kaufman. *Creating Social Change*. New York: Holt, Rinehart & Winston, Incorporated, 1972.

Articles

Ackerman, Robert W. "How Companies Respond to Social Demands." *Harvard Business Review* 51 (July-August 1973): 88–98.

Anundsen, Kristin. "Management in the Briarpatch: An Alternative to 'The System.'" An Interview with Michael Phillips. *Management Review* (February 1975): 24–30.

Blumber, Phillip I. "The Politicization of the Corporation." *The Business Lawyer* (July 1971): 1551–1587.

Bowers, Norman and M. Neil Browne. "Democratic Legitimacy and the Social Responsibility of Private Corporations." *Akron Business and Economic Review* 3 (Winter 1972): 9–12.

Bremer, Otto A. "Is Business the Source of New Social Values?" *Harvard Business Review* 49 (November/December 1971): 121–126.
The view is advanced that business is taking the place of the church and family as a service of value formation.

Briscoe, R. "Utopians in the Marketplace." *Harvard Business Review* 49 (September 1971): 4–6+.

Brooks, John. "The Marts of Trade: The Anti-Corporation." *The New Yorker* (October 9, 1971):
A discussion of outside pressures on business to change.

Byrom, Fletcher L. "Public Affairs, Private Business and People." *The Conference Board Record* 12 (May 1975): 52–56.

Cassell, Frank H. "The Corporation and Community." *Business Topics* 18 (Autumn 1970): 11–19.

Chastain, Clark E. "Corporate Accounting for Environmental Information." *Financial Executive* (May 1975): 45–50.

Childs, Preston B. "Business: Society's Servant or Master?" *Personnel Journal* 54 (March 1975): 167–168, 178.

Cohen, Kalman J. and Richard M. Cyert. "Strategy: Formulation, Implementation, and Monitoring." *The Journal of Business* 46 (November 3, 1973): 352+.
The organization and the environment are parts of a complex interactive system.

Collier, Barnard Law. "The Badness of Bigness and the Bigness of Badness." *Saturday Review* 54 (June 12, 1971): 23–25.
Reviews of two books on corporations and their domination of American life: *America, Inc.,* by Morton Mintz and Jerry S. Cohen; and *Invisible Empires,* by Louis Turner.

Conrad, Alfred F. "The Corporate Machinery for Hearing and Heeding New Voices." *The Business Lawyer* (November 1971): 197–208.
A discussion of wider representation in corporate decisions.

"Corporate Social Policy in a Dynamic Society." *California Management Review* 15 (Summer 1973): 67–109.

Crotty, Philip T. "The Professional Manager of the Future." *Management of Personnel Quarterly* 10 (Fall 1971): 4–9.

Davis, Keith and Robert L. Blomstrom. "Adapting the Organization for Social Response." *Arizona Business* 22 (June/July 1975): 12–16.

Day, Virgil B. "Business Priorities in a Changing Environment." *Journal of General Management* 1 (November 1, 1973):
As societal & national goals change so too will the social charter of the corporation.

Epstein, E.M. "Dimensions of Corporate Power." *California Management Review* 16 (Winter 1973): 19–23.

"Executives Tell Why It's Harder and Harder to Run a Company!" *US News and World Report* 73 (October 2, 1972): 74–77.

Headaches for corporate managers seem endless; they range from expanding government controls to demands for greater social responsibility.

Fuqua, J. B. "Can There Be Corporate Democracy?" *Public Relations Journal* 29 (April 1973): 10–12.

Gavin, J. M. "Will the Corporation Continue as a Leader in Our Changing Society?" *Financial Executive* 39 (June 1971): 30–32+.

Gerber, William. "Changing Corporate World.: *Editorial Research Reports* (February 3, 1971): 83–99.

Greenwood, William T. "Business in Reaction to Social Pressures." *The Conference Board Record* 12 (May 1975): 46–49.

Hoover, John Edgar. "The Extremist-Terrorist Demand: A Death Sentence for Industry?" *Finance* 89 (May 1971): 16–19.

"I Don't Think We Can Afford to Refer to Corporations as Private Enterprise Anymore." *Forbes* 110 (November 1972): 50–52.

"Interview: Eugene McCarthy on Professionalism and Corporate Responsibility." *Master in Business Administration* 6 (October 1971): 54–55.

"Key Question This Year: Is Your Business on a Collision Course with the Public?" *Business Management* 39 (January 1971): 37–40.

Kinney, R. J. "Corporate Response to Social Challenge." *Public Relations Journal* 27 (August 1971): 13–15+.

Kozmetsky, G. "How Much Revolution Does American Business Need?" *Conference Board Record* 8 (March 1971): 17–20.

Kuhn, James. "Business and Its Publics." *Christianity and Crisis* 32 (February 7, 1972): 9–13.

Lawrence, F. G. "Can Industry Get the Public in Its Corner?" *Industry Week* 177 (May 14, 1973): 30–34+.

Lazer, William, John F. Smallwood and others. "Consumer Environments and Life Styles of the Seventies." *MSU Business Topics* 20 (Spring 1972): 5–17.

MacNamee, Holly. "Business Leadership in Social Change: Philosophy, Communications, and the Local Level." *Conference Board Record* 8 (July 1971): 25–32.

McAfee, Jerry. "Industry's Response to Its Social Responsibilities." *Canadian Welfare* 47 (January/February 1971): 10–12+.

McAlmon, George A. "The Corporate Boardroom: A Closed Circle." *Business and Society Review* 12 (Winter 1974–75): 65–71.

McFarland, Dalton E. "Management and Its Critics." *Journal of Business Research* 2 (October 1974): 395–408.

McGuire, Joseph W. "Business and the Generation Gap." *California Management Review* 13 (Winter 1970): 78–88.

Maruer, John C. "Rational Management Responses to External Effects." *Academy of Management Journal* (March 1971): 99–115.

Michaelis, Michael. "The Management of Change." *The Futurist V* (February 1971): 9–11.
In the future corporation managers will have to remodel their organizations on basis of needs of society, including ethical values of a global technology.

Mitchell, A. "Changing Values." *International Advertiser* 12 (Winter 1971): 5–9.

Mee, John F. "The Mission of the Business Firm." *Miami Business Review* 42 (June 1971): 1–4.

Monsen, R. Joseph. "The Unrecognized Social Revolution: The Rise of the New Business Elite in America." *California Management Review* 14 (Winter 1971): 13–17.

Mushrock, M.J. "GM—Power to the People?" *Automotive Industry* 144 (February 1, 1971): 18–19.

Oates, D. "Is Company Loyalty Dead?" *International Management* 29 (November 1974): 12–16.

Passer, Harold C. "As Profits Rise—What to Say to Critics of Business." *Association Management* 24 (May 1972): 64–68.
The author argues the importance of presenting the social benefits of the profit system.

103

Preston, Lee and James E. Post. "The Third Managerial Revolution." *Academy of Management Journal* 17 (September 1974): 476–486.
    The authors discuss the gradual shift to participative behavior in management decision making as a response to social expectations and changes.

"Radicals in the Boardrooms?" *Forbes* 109 (May 15, 1972): 61–65.

Raymond, R. S. and E. Richards. "Social Indicators and Business Decisions." *MSU Business Topics* 19 (Autumn 1971): 42–46.

Rich, Stuart U. "Meeting the Challenge of Change." *Oregon Business Review* 30 (February 1971): 1+.
    A discussion of major problems facing the US during the seventies. Why these problems loom so large today and what role corporations must play in helping to solve them.

Rockefeller, David. "Business Must Perform Better." *Wall Street Journal* 178 (December 21, 1971): 10.

Ross, Douglas N. "Business Confronts Itself at the 'Credibility Gap'—And Agrees There's Reason for It to Look Before Leaping to a Conclusion." *Conference Board Record* 10 (July 1973): 24–27.
    This contains the chief findings of the conference board's survey of business opinion and experience in which 123 business executives were asked to discuss implications for business of recent public polls, and to assess what might be done to raise corporate ratings.

Sawyer, George C. "Social Issues and Social Change: Impact on Strategic Decisions." *MSU Business Topics* 21 (Summer 1973): 15–20.

Sayers, Wilson B. "The Future of Business in American Society." *The Futurist* V (February 1971): 15.
    Sayers reviews an article by Eli Goldston, "Perspectives on Business," *Daedalus* (Winter 1969), in which he says in the future business firms wil take social responsibility more seriously, will be more open to public scrutiny.

Schwartz, Donald E. "Towards New Corporate Goals: Co-existence with Society." *Georgetown Law Journal* 60 (October 1971): 57–109.

Schwartz, Kenneth. "How Social Activists See Business." *Business and Society Review* 14 (Summer 1975): 70–73.

Stabler, Charles N. "Changing Times: For Many Corporations Social Responsibility Is Now a Major Concern. *The Wall Street Journal* 178 (October 26, 1971): 1+.

Starr, Roger. "Power and the People—The Case of Con Edison." *The Public Interest* (Winter 1972): 75+.

Twedt, D. W. "Society and Management: Where Do We Go from Here?" *Administrative Management* 36 (January 1975): 22–23.

VanArsdell, Paul M. "The Business Corporation: Limited or Unlimited." *Southern Journal of Business* 7 (May 1972): 1–10.

Vanderwicken, Peter. "Change Invades the Boardroom." *Fortune* 85 (May 1972): 156–159+.

Vanderwicken, Peter. "GM: The Price of Being Responsible." *Fortune* 85 (January 1972): 98–101+.
    Profits have been lagging despite record sales, and there is a question whether the new social and environmental demands on the company—which it is determined to meet—have fundamentally affected the prospects of a great American "Money Machine."

Ways, Max. "Crisis of Success: Material or Mental?" *Conference Board Record* 8 (July 1971): 36–37.

Ways, Max. "It Isn't a Sick Society." *Fortune* 84 (December 1971): 100–103+.

White, Arthur H. "Changing Rules of the Game in the American Marketplace." *Public Relations Journal* (October 1973): 6–8.

Williamson, Oliver. "Markets and Hierarchies: Some Elementary Considerations." *The American Economic Review* 63 (1973): 316–325. A discussion of changing management transactions and organizational developments.

Yankelovich, Daniel, Inc., Corporate Priorities: A Continuing Study of the New Demands on Business." *A Brochure* Stamford, Connecticut, 1972.

Consumerism

Books

Aaker, David A. and George S. Day, eds. *Consumerism: Search for the Consumer Interest* (2nd edition). New York: The Free Press, 1974.

Andreasen, Alan R. *The Disadvantaged Consumer*. New York: The Free Press, 1975.
    This book focuses on the problem of the economically disadvantaged minority consumer with an attempt at making some positive public policy proposals.

Bruce, Ronald, ed. *The Consumer's Guide to Product Safety*. New York: Award Books, 1971.

Cohen, Manuel Frederick and George J. Stigler. *Can Regulatory Agencies Protect Consumers?* Washington: American Enterprise Institute for Public Policy Research, 1971.

Consumerism: New Developments for Business. Chicago: Commerce Clearing House, 1971.

Consumerism: Things Ralph Nader Never Told You by the editors of *Fortune*. New York: Harper & Row, 1973, c1972.

Cron, Rodney L. *Assuring Customer Satisfaction*. New York: Van Nostrand Reinhold Company, 1974.
    Guide for business and industry.

Faber, Doris. *Enough! The Revolt of the American Consumer*. New York: Farrar, Straus and Giroux, 1972.

Faure, Edgar. *The Heart of the Battle: For a New Social Contract*. New York: McGraw-Hill, 1972.
    Translated from French by Gill Manning.

Gaedeke, Ralph M. and Warren W. Etcheson, comps. *Consumerism*. San Francisco: Canfield Press, 1972.
    Viewpoints from business, government, and the public interest.

Gartner, Alan and Frank Riessman. *The Service Society and the Consumer Vanguard*. 1st edition. New York: Harper & Row, 1974.

Goble, Ross L. and Roy T. Shaw, comp. *Controversy and Dialogue in Marketing*. Englewood Cliffs, N.J.: Prentice-Hall, 1974, c1975.

Hapgood, David. *The Screwing of the Average Man*. 1st edition. Garden City, New York: Doubleday, 1974.
    On Consumer protection.

Haskins, James. *The Consumer Movement*. New York: F. Watts, 1975.
    Describes the growing movement for consumer protection and stresses the importance of being an intelligent consumer.

106

In the Marketplace edited by editors of *Ramparts* with Frank Browning. San Francisco: Canfield Press, 1972.
Consumerism in America discussed.

Jelley, Herbert M. and Robert O. Herrmann. *The American Consumer: Issues and Decisions.* New York: Gregg Division, McGraw-Hill, 1973.

Keeton, Page and Marshall S. Shapo. *Products and the Consumer: Deceptive Practices.* Mineola, New York: Foundation Press, 1972.

Kelley, William Thomas, ed. *New Consumerism: Selected Readings.* Columbus, Ohio: Grid, Incorporated, 1973.
Consumers, Industry-social aspects consumer protection.

Lasson, Kenneth. *Proudly We Hail: Profiles of Public Citizens in Action.* New York: Grossman Publishers, 1975.
Consumer protection-Unted States case studies.

Murray, Barbara B., ed. *Consumerism, the Eternal Triangle.* Pacific Palisades, California: Goodyear Publishing Company, 1973.
Business, government and consumers.

Nadel, Mark V. *The Politics of Consumer Protection.* Indianapolis: Bobbs-Merrill, 1971.

Nader, Ralph, ed. *The Consumer and Corporate Accountability.* New York: Harcourt Brace Jovanovich, 1973.

Oppenheim, Saul C. and Glen E. Weston. *Unfair Trade Practices and Consumer Protection* 3rd edition. St. Paul: West Publishing Company, 1974.
Cases and comments—consumer protection, unfair competition.

Rosefsky, Robert S. *Frauds, Swindles, and Rackets.* Chicago: Follett Publishing Company, 1973.
Red alert for today's consumers.

Sanford, David. *Who Put the Con in Consumer?* New York: Liveright, 1972.
Consumer protection, education.

Schrag, Philip G. *Counsel for the Deceived.* 1st edition. New York: Pantheon Books, 1972.
Case studies in consumer fraud.

Shapiro, Howard S. *How to Keep Them Honest.* Emmaus, Pa.: Rodale Press, 1974.

Herbert Denenberg on spotting the professional phonies, unscrewing insurance and protecting your interests.

Swagler, Roger. *Caveat Emptor: An Introductory Analysis of Consumer Problems.* Lexington, Massachusetts: D.C. Heath & Company, 1975.

Taylor, Jack Lawrence, Jr. and Arch W. Troelstrup, comps. *The Consumer in American Society.* New York: McGraw-Hill, 1974.

Winter, Ralph K., Jr. *The Consumer Advocate Versus the Consumer.* Washington: American Enterprise Institute for Public Policy Research, 1972.

Withers, William. *The Corporations and Social Change. Woodbury,* New York: Barron's Educational Series, Incorporated, 1972.

Articles

Aaker, David A. and George S. Day. "Corporate Responses to Consumerism Pressures." *Harvard Business Review* 50 (November/December 1972): 114–124.
    Despite internal barriers and external threats, companies and trade associations are making progress with action programs.

Anderson, Ralph E. and Joseph F. Hair. "Consumerism: A Force to Be Reconciled." *Mississippi Business Review* 33 (April 1972): 3–9.

Anderson, Ralph E. and Marvin A. Jolson. "Consumer Expectations and the Communications Gap: Causes of Consumer Dissatisfaction." *Business Horizons* 16 (April 1973): 11–16.

Anderson, W. Thomas and William H. Cunningham. "Socially Conscious Consumer." *Journal of Marketing* 36 (July 1972): 23–31.

"The Angry Consumer: No Words Can Express My Disgust." *US News and World Report* 77 (July 15, 1974): 42–44.

Armstrong, Richard. "Passion That Rules Ralph Nader." *Fortune* 83 (May 1971): 144–147+.

"Associations Answer Consumerism Challenge." *Association Management* 23 (January 1971): 24–27.

"Associations Confront the Critical Consumer." *Savings and Loan News* 92 (June 1971): 28–34.

Barksdale, Hiram C. and Warren A. French. "Response to Consumerism: How Change Is Perceived by Both Sides." *MSU Business Topics* 23 (Spring 1975): 55–67.
A call for improved performance and increased sensitivity.

Barksdale, Hiram C. and William K. Darden. "Consumer Attitudes Toward Marketing and Consumerism." *Journal of Marketing* 36 (October 1972): 22–35.

"BBB's Consumer Unit Seeks Funds, Local Help." *Advertising Age* 44 (March 26, 1973): 90.

Becker, Boris W. "Consumerism: A Challenge or a Threat?" *Journal of Retailing* 48 (Summer 1972): 16–28.

Berens, John S. "Consumer Costs in Product Failure." *MSU Business Topics* (Spring 1971): 27–30.
Although coverage is inadequate in many cases, progress is being made in administration of warranty policy.

Block, Joyanne E. "The Aged Consumer and the Market Place: A Critical Review." *Marquette Business Review* (Summer 1974): 73–81.

Blum, Milton L. and others. "Consumer Affairs: Viability of the Corporate Response." *Journal of Marketing* 38 (April 1974): 13–19.

Bogart, Leo. "Customers, Not Consumers." *Conference Board Record* 9 (May 1972): 34–37.

Borson, Robert. "Showdown at the Cash Register: Special Report." *Pacific Business* 61 (May/June 1971): 17–24.
What business is doing to resolve the consumer's legitimate concern over the workings of the marketplace.

Brunk, Max E. "The Anatomy of Consumerism." *Freeman* 23 (February 1973): 78–84. [also Journal of Advertising 2 (November 1, 1973): 9–11+].

Burck, Gilbert. "High-Pressure Consumerism at the Salesman's Door." *Fortune* 86 (July 1972): 70+.
Possibility of "regulatory-monster"?

Bytin, James E. "Fixing the Fixers." *Wall Street Journal.* 179 (January 11, 1972): 1+.
Carney, James A. "Section 5 of the Federal Trade Commission Act—

Unfairness to Consumers." *Wisconsin Law Review* 4 (1972): 1071–1096.

Carpenter, James W. "Consumer Protection in Ohio Against False Advertising and Deceptive Practices." *Ohio State Law Journal* 32 (Winter 1971): 1–15.

"Challenge of Product Safety." *Research Management* 18 (March 1975): 12–25.

Cohen, Dorothy. "Remedies for Consumer Protection: Prevention, Restitution, or Punishment." *Journal of Marketing* 39 (October 1975): 24–31.

"Consumer Laws Can Aid Industry, Too." *Industry Week* 176 (January 29, 1973): 55–56.

"Consumer Protection." *Canadian Labour* (September 1971). (Entire issue on this topic).

"Consumer Protection." *Congressional Quarterly Weekly Report* 29 (February 5, 1971): 320–322.

"Consumerism and the Product Hazard." *Journal of Insurance* 35 (January/February 1974): 13–28.
  Highlights from symposium sponsored by Insurance Information Institute and American Society of Insurance Management. Dallas, Texas, 1973.

"Consumerism: Better Business Bureaus Rate Gripes." *Sales Management* 109 (August 21, 1972): 3.

"Consumerism Moves In-House." *Industry Week* 173 (June 5, 1972): 36–40.
  Involves workforces in quality control efforts.

"Consumers Battle at the Grass Roots." *Business Week* (February 26, 1972): 86+.

"Consumers Fighting Back via Better Business Bureaus: Customers' Complaints About Products and Services Are Spiraling." *US News* 73 (December 18, 1972): 58+.
  Survey of what's bothering people and one way business is responding.

Day, George S. and David A. Aaker. "A Guide to Consumerism." *Journal of Marketing* (July 1970): 15.

110

"A Dollar's Worth." *American Association of University Women Journal* 65 (April 1972): 1–18.

"Drive to Protect the Buyer." *U.S. News and World Report* 70 (January 18, 1971): 20–21.

Dunsing, Marilyn M. "Consumerism: Protection, Information, and Education." *Business Review* 29 (May 1972): 6–8.

Evaldi, Thomas L. and Gestrin, Joan E. "Justice for Consumers." *Northwestern University Law Review* 66 (July/August 1971): 281–325.

Ferguson, John R. "Consumer Ignorance as a Source of Monopoly Power." *Antitrust Law and Economics Review* 5 (Winter 1971/72): 79–102; (Spring 1972): 55–74.

Fraser, Edie. "Consumer Legislative Update." *Business and Society Review* 12 (Winter 1974–75): 58–63.

Gaedeke, Ralph M. and U. Udo-Aka. "Toward the Internationalization of Consumerism." *California Management Review* 17 (Fall 1974): 86–92.

Gray, Elisha II. "It's Later than You Think." *American Gas Association Monthly* (December 1972): 20.

Green, Mark J. "Appropriatiness and Responsiveness: Can the Government Protect the Consumer?" *Journal of Economic Issues* 8 (June 1974): 309–328.

Greyser, Stephen A. "Marketing and Responsiveness to Consumerism." *Journal of Contemporary Business* (Autumn 1973): 81–94.

Greyser, Stephen A. and Steven L. Diamond. "Business Is Adapting to Consumerism." *Harvard Business Review* 52 (September 1974): 38–58.

Grikscheit, Gary and Kent L. Granzin. "Who Are the Consumerists?" *Journal of Business Research* 3 (January 1975): 1–12.

Grotta, Daniel. "The Ralph Nader of Insurance." Saturday Review of the Society 55 (July 1, 1972): 34–41.
Pennsylvania's insurance commissioner, Herbert L. Denenberg, protects the consumer.

"Help for Consumers on the Way." *U.S. News and World Report* 71 (November 15, 1971): 34.

111

Hendon, Donald W. "Toward a Theory of Consumerism." *Business Horizons* 18 (August 1975): 16–24.

Hollier, Derek. "Does a Consumerism Crunch Threaten Business?" *Business Administration* (January 1973): 21–23.
  British Business should learn a lesson from the United States and come to terms with consumerism—even to profit from it.

Hussey, E. O. "Developing and Marketing a Safe Product." *Research Management* 18 (March 1975): 20–22.
  A discussion of flame retardant sleepwear.

Ignatov, Alexander. "Those Unfortunate Consumers." *New Times* (Moscow) 28 (July 1972): 28–30.
  Some emphasis on the contributions of Ralph Nader to the United States consumer protection movement.

"Interview with Ralph Nader: A Progress Report on Consumer Issues." *US News and World Report* 79 (October 27, 1975): 26–29.

Jeffries, James D. "Protection for Consumers Against Unfair and Deceptive Business." *Marquette Law Review* 57 (November 4, 1974): 559–606.

Johnson, Jimmy D. "Consumerism: The Case—And Care—for Frustration." *Association Management* 26 (June 1974): 95–99.

Jolson, Marvin A. "Cooling Off the Door-to-Door Salesman." *Business and Economic Dimensions* 7 (February 1971): 7–17.

Jones, Mary Gardiner and Barry B. Boyer. "Improving the Quality of Justice in the Marketplace: The Need for Better Consumer Remedies." *George Washington Law Review* 40 (March 1972): 357–415.

Kahalas, Harvey. "The Problem and Challenges of Consumerism." *Akron Business and Economic Review* (Summer 1974): 20–25.

Kangun, Norman and Keith K. Cox, James Higginbotham, John Burton. "Consumerism and Marketing Management." *Journal of Marketing* 39 (April 1975): 3–10.

Kaufman, Ira and Derek Channon. "International Consumerism: A Threat or Opportunity?" *Industrial Marketing Management* 3 (October 1973): 1–12.
  Examples of consumerism and corporate strategy in Europe, Great Britain and the United States.

112

Kotler, Philip. "How to Anticipate Consumerism's Coming Threat to Banking." *Banking* 65 (January 1973): 20–22.

Why banks have fared well so far and how the industry can respond to criticism of various banking practices.

Kotler, Philip. "What Consumerism Means for Marketer." *Business Review* 50 (May/June 1972): 48–57.

The challenge for business is to develop products and marketing practices that combine short- and long-run consumer values.

Layton, R. A. and G. Holmes. "Consumerism as an Element of On-Going Social Change." *Management Decision* 12 (November 5, 1975): 313–328.

McHugh, Helen F. "Consumer Protection Against—What?" *Journal of Home Economics* 64 (May 1972): 14–17.

Margolius, Sidney. "Consumer's Needs Persist." *American Federationist* 78 (January 1971): 1–6.

Margolius, Sidney. "What's Worrying the Consumer?" *American Federationist* 81 (March 1974): 19–21.

Markin, Ron J. "Consumerism: Militant Consumer Behavior." *Business & Society* 12 (Fall 1971): 5–17.

Social and behavioral analysis.

Maynes, E. Scott. "Power of Consumers." *Business Horizons* 15 (June 1972): 77–86.

Michman, Ronald D. "Impact of Consumerism: A Response Needed in Product Planning." *Business & Economic Dimensions* 9 (May/June 1973): 7–11.

Mitchell, Jeremy. "The Consumer Movement and Technological Change." *International Social Science Journal* 25 (November 3, 1973): 358–369.

Morin, Bernard A. "Consumerism Revisited." *MSU Business Topics* 19 (Summer 1971): 47–51.

Murphy, Pat and Ben M. Enis. "Let's Hear the Case Against Brand X." *Business and Society Review* (Winter 1974–1975): 82–89.

Nader, Ralph. "The Dossier Invades the Home." *Saturday Review* 54 April 17, 1971): 18–21, 58–59.

An exposé on how credit bureaus and inspection agencies collect private information about many citizens on which there are no legal restrictions as to who else can see it.

"Naderism Spreads Its Wings." *Economist* 239 (May 29, 1971): 49–51.

"New Help For Shoppers, Tighter Rules for Business." *U.S. News and World Report* 70 (March 8, 1971): 68–69.

"A New Kind of Consumer Watchdog." *Business Week* (July 22, 1972): 42–43.

Palmer, H. Bruce. "Consumerism: The Business of Business." *Michigan Business Review* 23 (July 1971): 12–17.
The role of the new council of better business bureaus.

Peterson, Mary B. "How Consumerism Backfires." *Nation's Business* 60 (May 1972): 30–31.

Pfister, Richard L. "A Plea for a Sane Energy Policy." *Business Horizons* 18 (June 1975): 59–64.

Pollock, Francis. "Consumer Reporting." *Columbia Journalism Review* 10 (May/June 1971): 37–43.

Primeaux, Walter J. "Consumerism: A Challenge to Business." *Mississippi's Business* 31 (December 1972): 1–6.

"Protecting and Preserving Consumer Integrity Main Aim of Business." *Commerce Today* 3 (November 27, 1972): 23.

Pruden, Henry O. and Douglas S. Longman. "Race, Alienation, and Consumerism." *Journal of Marketing* 36 (July 1972): 58–63.
Reply with rejoinder. E. L. Landon, Jr. and W. J. Lundstrom. *Journal of Marketing* 37 (April 1973): 67–70.

Rosenberg, Larry J. "Retailers' Responses to Consumerism." *Business Horizons* 19 [18] (October 1975): 37–44.

Rosenberg, Mark L. "Class Actions for Consumer Protection." *Harvard Civil Rights—Civil Liberties Law Review* 7 (May 1972): 601–629.

Scherf, Gerhard W. H. "Consumer Education as a Means of Alleviating Dissatisfaction." *The Journal of Consumer Affairs* (Summer 1974): 61–75.

Schrag, Philip G. "Consumer Rights." *Columbia Forum* 13 (Summer, 1970): 4–10.

Schrag, Philip G. "On Her Majesty's Secret Service." *Yale Law Journal* 80 (July 1971): 1529–1603.

Shafer, Harold. "Consumerism and Retailing: Let's Restore the Balance." *Canadian Business* 47 (April 1974): 10–13.

Sheth, Jagdish N. and Nicholas J. Mammana. "Recent Failures in Consumer Protection." *California Management Review* 16 (Spring 1974): 64–72.

Sommer, A. A. "Random Thoughts on Disclosure as 'Consumer' Protection." *Business Lawyer* 27 (November 1971): 85–91.

"Special Issue on Consumerism." *Journal of Retailing* 48 (Winter 1972–1973): 3–100.

Stern, Louis L. "Consumer Protection via Self-Regulation." *Journal of Marketing* 35 (July 1971): 47–53.

Synder, James D. "Those (Expletive Deleted) Consumerists—What Are They Planning Next?" *Sales Management* 112 (May 27, 1974): 18–22.

Thain, Gerald J. "Consumer Protection Advertising—the FTC Response." *Business Lawyer* 27 (April 1972): 891–906.

"Truth in Packaging—Consumer Affairs." *California Journal* 3 (June/July 1972): 192–195.

"Upholding the Interests of the Consumer." *OECD Observer* 63 (April 1973): 5–7.

Walker, Orville C. and others. "The Potential Secondary Effects of Consumer Legislation: A Conceptual Framework." *Journal of Consumer Affairs* 8 (Winter 1974): 144–156.

Wasem, George. "Marketing and Consumerism—Are They Compatible?" *Bankers Monthly Magazine* (January 15, 1973): 20–23.

Webster, Frederick E. Jr. "Does Business Misunderstand Consumerism?" 51 *Harvard Business Review* (September-October 1973): 89–93.

West, Michael G. "Disclaimer of Warranties—Its Curse and Possible Cure." *Journal of Consumer Affairs* 5 (Winter 1971): 154–173.

Willenborg, John F. "The Emergence of Consumerism as a Social Force." *Business and Economic Review* 18 (December 1971): 2–6.

Wood, Roberta A. "The Consumer Credit Protection Act: An Analysis of Public Policy Formulation." *Journal of Consumer Affairs* 5 (Winter 1971): 196–211.

Worsnop, Richard L. "Directions of the Consumer Movement." *Editorial Research Reports* (January 12, 1972): 23–40.

Wotruba, Thomas R. and Patricia L. Duncan. "Are Consumers Really Satisfied?" *Business Horizons* 18 (February 1975): 85–90.

Credibility Crisis and the Fallen Image of Business

Articles

"The American Corporation Under Fire." *Newsweek* (May 24, 1971): 74+.

"Americans Are Pro-business, Wattenberg Says." *Advertising Age* 45 (December 16, 1974): 36–38.

"America's Growing Antibusiness Mood." *Business Week* (June 17, 1972): 100–103.
   A report on public attitudes toward business.

Barnet, Rosalind C. and Renato Tagiuri. "What Young People Think About Managers." *Harvard Business Review* 51 (May-June 1973): 106–118.

Bell, Daniel. "The Corporation and Society in the 1970's." *The Public Interest* 24 (Summer 1971): 5–32.
   Discusses changing attitudes towards the corporation over the years, new criticisms of it from ecological and public interest viewpoints. Economic and social obligations and responsibilities of the corporation are discussed.

Benham, Thomas W. "Restoring Public Confidence in Business." *Financial Executive* 42 (February 1974): 36–40.

Bennett, K. W. "Public Image of Business Continues to Sag." *Iron Age* 210 (November 9, 1972): 52–53.

Brown, Paul I. "Business vs. the Public: Why Protest Doesn't Work." *Management Review* 65 (March 1976): 4–10.

Burke, M. C. and L. L. Berry. "Do Social Actions of a Corporation Influence Store Image and Profits?" *Journal of Retailing* 50 (Winter 1974–1975): 62–72.

"Business Takes on Its Critics." *U.S. News and World Report* 70 (April 26, 1971): 52–54.

Chandler, M. "Corporate Crownthorns or Laurels?" *Public Utilities* 88 (August 19, 1971): 24–29.

Foster, E. and G. Bull. "Reputation of Business." *The Director; Journal of the Institute of Directors* 26 (November 1973): 270–275.

Goodman, Stanley J. "Raising the Fallen Image of Business." Address at Opening Luncheon, National Retail Merchants Association, New York—January 7, 1974.
A description of the drop in the reputation of business and a call to higher ethical standards and greater responsiveness to the external publics.

Hamilton, Walter A. "On the Credibility of Institutions." *Conference Board Record* 10 (March 1973): 33–38.

Hieronymus, William S., Jr. "Restoring Faith: Worried About Image, Business Makes Effort to Sell Itself to Public." *Wall Street Journal* 181 (June 12, 1973): 1+.

Hobbing, Enno. "Business Must Explain Itself." *Business and Society Review* 3 (Autumn 1972): 85–86.

"How Business Faces a Hostile Climate." *Business Week* (September 16, 1972): 70–72.

Juster, Jacqueline. "Public Opinion of Business: There's a Gap in Communication." *New Jersey Business* 20 (September 1973): 36–39+.
What some New Jersey firms are doing to rectify the situation.

Lerner, Max. "The Shame of the Professions." *Saturday Review* (November 1, 1975): 10–12.
Introductory article to special report on corruption in government, business, medicine, and other professions.

Lewis, Marshall C. "How Business Can Escape the Climate of Mistrust." *Business and Society Review* (Winter 1975-76): 70–71.
The author sets forth a six point strategy for restoring confidence in business.

McGrath, Phyllis S. "Managing Corporate External Relations: Changing Perspectives and Responses. A Research Report by the *Conference Board* 679, New York, New York. January 1976.

An analysis of corporate relations in the context of ethical and credibility crisis.

Melloan, George. "Business Morality and Its Vocal Critics." *Wall Street Journal* 178 (August 26, 1971): 10.

"Negative Business Image Draws Worldwide Concern." *Industry Week* 170 (September 13, 1971): 13–14+.

"Public Dissent and Professional Responsibility." *Civil Engineering* 43 (September 1973): 98–99.

"Public Is Sour on Business—And That Opinion Is Worsening." *Industry Week* 173 (June 12, 1972): 26+.

Rafe, S. C. "Credibility—Key to Communications Success." *Public Relations Journal* 28 (June 1972): 14–17.

Roche, James. "The Attack on Free Enterprise." *Michigan Business Review* (July 1971): 18+.

Rockefeller, David. "The Era of Growing Business Accountability." An address before the Advertising Council, New York (December 3, 1971).

Schwartz, Kenneth. "How Social Activists See Business." *Business and Society Review* (Summer 1975): 70–73.
    A report based on good empirical evidence—done by the Opinion Research Corporation in Princeton, New Jersey.

Seelye, Alfred L. "Societal Change and Business—Government Relationships." *MSU Business Topics* 23 (Autumn 1975): 5–11.
    Declining confidence in business can be stemmed only by positive programs and attitudes.

"Survey Reveals Deep-Rooted Antibusiness Attitudes in U.S." *Industry Week* 186 (September 1, 1975): 12–13.

Tribus, Myron. "Technology and Society—The Real Issues." *Bulletin of the Atomic Scientists* (December 1971).
    Leaders of business and government who control technology are not trusted by the public.

Ways, Max. "Business Needs to Do a Better Job of Explaining Itself." *Fortune* (September 1972): 85–87, 192, 196, 198.

Ecology: Physical Environment and Energy

Books

Adelman, M. A. *The World Petroleum Market.* Baltimore: The Johns Hopkins Press, 1972.
Contrary to most experts the author argues that rather than a shortage of oil there is an excess.

Allvine, Fred C. and James M. Patterson. *Competition, LTD.: The Marketing of Gasoline.* Bloomington, Indiana: Indiana University Press, 1972.
A plea for the restructuring of the petroleum industry in the interest of greater business competition.

Berry, Mary Clay. *The Alaska Pipeline.* Bloomington, Indiana: Indiana University Press, 1975.
Written from an environmentalist perspective the author attacks the oil industry as she tells the story of the pipeline.

Buggie, Frederick D. and Richard Gurman. *Toward Effective and Equitable Pollution Control Regulation.* New York: American Management Associations, 1972.

Campbell, Rex R. and Jerry L. Wade. *Society and Environment.* Boston: Allyn and Bacon, 1972.

Chatham, George N. and Franklin P. Huddle. *The Supersonic Transport.* Washington, D.C.: Library of Congress, February 26, 1971.

Commoner, Barry. *The Closing Circle.* New York: Knopf, 1971.

Cross, Frank L., ed. *Management Primer on Water Pollution Control.* Westport, Connecticut: Technomic Company, Inc., 1975.
A technical approach to the two principal types of water pollution—municipal wastes and industrial wastes—and the various remedial possibilities.

Davies, J. Clarence, III. *The Politics of Pollution.* New York: Pegasus, 1971.

Downs, Anthony, et. al. *The Political Economy of Environmental Control.* Berkeley, California: Institute of Business and Economic Research, University of California, 1972.

Edmunds, S. and John Letey. *Environmental Administration.* New York: McGraw-Hill, 1973.

Ehrlich, Paul R., Anne H. Ehrlich and John P. Holdren. *Human Ecology: Problems and Solutions.* San Francisco: W. H. Freeman & Company, 1973.

Goldman, Marshall, ed. *Controlling Pollutions: The Economics of a Cleaner America.* Englewood Cliffs, New Jersey: Prentice-Hall, 1972.

Goldstein, J. *How To Manage Your Company Ecologically.* New York: Rodale Press, 1971.

Heilbroner, Robert. *An Inquiry into the Human Prospect.* New York: W. W. Norton, 1974.
A gloomy prospect in light of increasing population and decreasing carrying capacity unless we change our life style and alter our political and economic system.

Henry, Harold W. *Pollution Control: Corporate Response.* New York: American Management Associations, 1974.
A briefing.

Johnson, Warren A. and John Hardesty, eds. *Economic Growth vs. the Environment.* Belmont, California: Wadsworth, 1971.

Kneese, Allen V. and Charles L. Schultze. *Pollution, Prices and Public Policy. Washington, D.C.:* The Brookings Institute, 1975.

Meadows, Dennis L. *The Limits to Growth.* New York: Universe Books, 1972.
The results and draconian predictions of the club of Rome studies.

Reed, Charles B. *Fuels, Minerals and Human Survival: An Inquiry Concerning the Future of Our Industrial Society.* Ann Arbor, Michigan: Ann Arbor Science Publishers, 1975.

Ridgeway, James. *The Last Play: The Struggle to Monopolize the World's Energy Resources.* New York: E. P. Dutton & Company, 1973.
A description of how oil companies destroy competition. It is a valuable guide to the energy industry.

Rodgers, William. *Brownout: The Power Crisis in America.* New York: Stein and Day, 1972.
A history of the electrical power industry in America with an indictment of both business and government.

120

Toward a New Environmental Ethic. Booklet No. 5500-0031. Washington, D.C.: Office of Public Affairs, U.S. Environmental Protection Agency, 1973.

Willrich, Mason. *Energy and World Politics.* New York: Free Press, 1975.

Articles

Alberts, David S. and John Marshall Davis. "Decision-Making Criteria for Environmental Protection and Control." A paper for the 12th American Meeting of the Institute of Management Sciences, Detroit (October 1971).

Alexander, Michael O. and J. Leslie Livingstone. "What Are the Real Costs and Benefits of Producing 'Clean' Electric Power?" *Public Utilities Fortnightly* 92 (August 30, 1973): 15–19.

Alexander, Tom. "The Big Blowup over Nuclear Blowdowns." *Fortune* (May 1973): 216+.

Anderson, W. Thomas, Jr., Louis K. Sharpe, and Robert J. Boewadt. "The Environmental Role for Marketing." *MSU Business Topics* 20 (Summer 1972): 66+.
    Products and procedures of the past are no longer appropriate; they have been invalidated by a shift in consumer priorities and goals.

"Are We Running Out of Energy and Capital? A Business Response to Barry Commoner." *Business and Society Review* 14 (Summer 1975): 46–49.

Baird, Bruce F. "Business and Our Environment." *Utah Economic and Business Review* 30 (November, 1970): 1–6.

Beams, Floyed A. and Paul E. Fertig. "Pollution Control Through Social Cost Conversion." *Journal of Accountancy* (November 1971): 37–42.

Bearse, A. W. "Air Pollution: A Case Study." *Management Accounting* 53 (September 1971): 16–18.

Beckerman, Wilfred. "The Myth of Finite Resources." *Business and Society Review* 16 (Winter 1974–75): 21–25.

An attack on the club of Rome report with attention to the moral issues.

Blumberg, Phillip I. "Corporate Responsibility and the Environment." *Conference Board Record* 8 (April 1971): 42–47.

Bowerman, Frank R. "Managing Solid Waste Disposal." *California Management Review* 14 (Spring 1972): 104–106.

Braaten, Carl E. "Caring for the Future: Where Ethics and Ecology Meet." *Zygon* 9 (December 1974): 311–322.

Bredewag, Harry W. "Showplace of Exploitation." *Engage/Social Action* 2 (June 1974): 28–33.

Brochi, Philip. "Economics and Ecology." *Ecologist* 1 (November 1971): 14–16.

Cain, Stanley A. "Environment—An All-Encompassing Phenomenon." Remarks at the 12th American Meeting of the Institute of Management Sciences, Detroit, October 2, 1971.

Caldwell, Lynton K. "Environmental Quality as an Administrative Problem." *The Annals of the American Academy of Political and Social Science* (March 1972): 108–115.

Cannon, James and Jean Halloran. "Steel and the Environment: A Long Way to Go." *Business and Society Review/Innovation* 4 (Winter 1972–73): 56–61.
    The council on Economic Priorities found that corporations and government agencies guarded information on pollution control jealously.

Carney, Marna K. and Frederick S. Carney. "Economics and Ethics of Pollution Control: An Interdisciplinary Analysis." *Soundings* 54 (Fall 1971): 271–287.
    An economist and ethicist come together to write about pollution control. A scholarly essay of high order.

"The Challenge of the Environment: A Primer on EPA's Statutory Authority." U.S. Environmental Protection Agency (December 1972).
    A brief description of all relevant acts with some interpretation.

Chambliss, H. D., Jr. "Ecology Will Continue as Major PR Problem." *Public Relations Journal* 27 (January 1971): 23+.

Chass, Robert L. "Air Pollution Control: The Case of Los Angeles County." *California Management Review* 14 (Spring 1972): 92–103.

Chastain, Clark E. "A New Role for Accountants: Accounting for Environmental Expenditures." *Business and Society Review* 14 (Fall 1973): 5–12.

Chastain, Clark E. "Corporate Accounting for Environmental Information." *Financial Executive* 43 (May 1975): 45–48+.

Council on Economic Priorities. "Paper Profits: Pollution Audit 1972." Economics Priorities Report (July-August 1971).

Cracco, F. and J. Rostenne. "Socio-Ecological Product." *MSU Business Topics* 19 (Summer 1971): 27–34.

Davis, Keith and Robert L. Blomstrom. "Observations on Ecology and Business Responsibility." *Arizona Business* 21 (March 1974): 19–26.

Day, J. W. "Closing the Credibility Gap in Environmental Control." *Business Management* 40 (June 1971): 29+.

Dilley, S. C. "Case of the Nebulous Numbers." *Harvard Business Review* 52 (November 1974): 42–44+.
Cost/Benefit analysis of environmental expenditures.

Downs, Anthony. "Up and Down with Ecology—the Issue-Attention Cycle." *The Public Interest* 28 (Summer 1972): 38–50.

Dudick, Thomas S. "Cost Accounting to Adapt to the Needs of Nuclear Energy Plants." *Management Advisor* 11 (March/April 1974): 15–21.

"Ecology and Excellence." *Humanist* 30 (November/December 1970): 8–15+, 21–24.

"Environmental-Ethics Panel Offers Views and Guidelines." *Chemical Engineering* 78 (March 8, 1971): 109–116.

Faltemayer, Edmund. "The Energy 'Joyride' Is Over." *Fortune* (September 1972): 90+.

Faltermayer, Edmund K. "We Can Afford Clean Air." *Fortune* (May 1972): 159–163.

Ferguson, G. R. "Environment and Management's Responsibilities." *SAM Advanced Management Journal* 37 (October 1972): 66–72.

Fox, Harold W. "Ecological Challenges to Marketing Strategies." *Baylor Business Studies* (February/March/April 1972): 2947.

Freeman, A. Myrick, III and Robert H. Haveman. "Clean Rhetoric and Dirty Water." *Public Interest* (Summer 1972): 51–65.

Gaede, William G. "Environmental Management Opportunities for the CPA." *Journal of Accountancy* 137 (May 1974): 50–54.

Gerber, Abrham. "Environment and the Energy Industries." *Business Economics* 6 (January 1971): 68–72.

Gunn, William N. "Packagers and the Environmental Challenge." *Harvard Business Review* 50 (July/August 1972): 103–111.

Hamrin, Robert. "Are Environmental Regulations Hurting the Economy." *Challenge* (May-June 1975): 29–38.

Hausknecht, Phillip A. "Anti-Pollution Struggle and Christian Responsibility." *The Japanese Christian Quarterly* 41 (Winter 1975): 18–24.

Kaufman, Irving R. "Power for the People—And by the People." *New York University Law Review* 46 (November 1971): 867–878.

Kavanagh, Preston B. "The New Environmental Ball Game." *Public Utilities Fortnightly* 86 (September 10, 1970): 25–31.

Kefalas, Asterios C. "The Management of Environmental Information: A Machine for Adapting a System to Its Environment." *A paper, the 12th American Meeting of the Institute for Management Science,* Detroit. September 29-October 2, 1971.

Klink, William H. "Environmental Concerns and the Need for a New Image of Man." *Zygon* 9 (December 1974): 300–310.

Kohn, R. E. "Price Elasticities of Demand and Air Pollution Control." *Review of Economics and Statistics* 54 (November 1972): 392–400.

"Leadtimes Foul Pollution Control." *Purchasing* 76 (January 22, 1974): 11+.

Leathers, Charles G. "New Dimensions of Countervailing Power Consumerism and Environmentalism." *MSU Business Topics* 20 (Winter 1972): 64–72.

McCullough, Harold. "The Death of a Mountain." *Engage/Social Action* 1 (March 1973): 24–31.

Describes the tremendous exploitation of land and people by strip mining.

McDonald, John. "Oil and the Environment: The Views from Maine." *Fortune* (April 1971): 84+.

McElroy, M. C. P. "Reckless Ecology Kick." *Marketing/Communications* 299 (September 1971): 33.

McIlvaine, R. W. "Air Pollution Control Involves Industrial Hygiene." *Foundry* 99 (October 1971): 74–77.

McKee, Jack Edward. "Water Pollution Control: A Task for Technology." *California Management Review* 14 (Spring 1972): 88–91.

Maucke, Richard B. "An Alternative Approach to Auto Emission Control." *California Management Review* 14 (Summer 1972): 82–86.

Meadows, Donella H. and Jorgen Randers. "The Carrying Capacity of the Globe." *Sloan Management Review* 13 (Winter 1972): 11–27.

Miller, H. "Environmental Complexity and Financial Reports." *Accounting Review* 47 (January 1972): 31–37.
Reply D.A. Wilson 48: 586–588 July 1973.

Moore, Michael L. and G. Fred Streuling. "Pollution Control Devices: Rapid Amortization Versus the Investment Credit." *Taxes* 52 (January 1974): 25–30.

Mulford, R. H. "Environmental Quality—A Challenge to Business." *Michigan Business Review* 23 (July 1971): 7–11+.

Myers, John G. "Energy Conservation and Economic Growth—Are They Incompatible?" *The Conference Board Record* 12 (February 1975): 27–32.

Obrzut, J. J. "Pollution Control Begins Inside the Plant." *Iron Age* 207 (January 28, 1971): 48–50.

Parker, J. E. "Accounting and Ecology: A Perspective." *The Journal of Accountancy* 132 (October 1971): 41–46.

"Paying for Pollution." *Municipal and Public Services Journal* 79 (June 18, 1971): 853–856+, 861–862.

Pen, J. "Seven Methods of Anti-Pollution Policy." *Economics Quarterly Review* (March 1971): 5–12.

"The Politics of Environmental Disruption." *Fortune* (January 1971): 69.

"Pollution and Industry." *U.S. News and World Report* 71 (November 22, 1971): 60–62.

Reichardt, Robert. "Dilemmas of Economic Behavior vis-à-vis Environmental Pollution." *Kyklos* 23 (1970): 849–865.

Rose, J. D. "Environmental Experts in the Chemical Industry." *Journal of Environmental Studies* 6 (February-March 1974): 167–171.

Sagan, L. A. "Human Costs of Nuclear Power." *Science* 177 (August 11, 1972): 487–493.

Schelling, Thomas C. "On the Ecology of Micromotives." *Public Interest* (Fall 1971): 59–98.

Sesser, Stanford N. "Changing Times: the Economy vs. the Environment." *Wall Street Journal* 178 (November 2, 1971): 1+.

Sherman, Howard and E. K. Hunt. "Pollution in Radical Perspective." *Business and Society Review* 3 (Autumn 1972): 48–53.
    Environmental catastrophe, more than class conflict, will be the undoing of American capitalism.

Simon, Herbert A. "Technology and the Environment." *Management Science* (June 1973): 1110–1121.

Sonde, Theodore and Harvey L. Pitt. "Utilizing the Federal Securities Laws to 'Clear the Air! Clean the Sky! Wash the Wind!'" *Harvard Law Journal* 16 (Summer 1971): 831–906.

Stahl, Sheldon W. "Social Cost—The Due Bill for Progress." *Monthly Review* Federal Reserve Bank of Kansas City (April 1972): 16+.
    A discussion of zero growth, pollution control and economic stability.

Stans, Maurice H. "Environment: Wait a Minute." *Wall Street Journal* 178 (August 6, 1971): 6.

Stinson, R. J. "Energy Crisis: Who Is Helped, Who Is Hurt?" *Financial World* 140 (November 28, 1973): 18–19+.

Stone, Richard. "The Evaluation of Pollution: Balancing Gains and Losses." *Minerva* 1 (July 1972): 412–425.

"Texaco's Continuing Environmental Work-in." *Texaco Star* 57 (No. 2, 1970): 2–7.

Thornton, Robert L. and Donald C. King. "Ecology—The Fear Appeal in the Public Sector." *MSU Business Topics* 20 (Winter 1972): 35–38.
> Future efforts to secure attention may prove ineffective if the scare technique has been overused in dealing with the pollution problem.

"Union Carbide: The Whole Truth?" [Environmental claims] *Business Week* (March 20, 1971): 27.

Wagner, L. E. "Environmental Pollution and Its Effect on the Financial Community." *Journal of Commercial Bank Lending* 52 (April 1972): 43–50.

Weickhardt, L. W. "Corporate Responsibility: The Environment." *Growth* (March 1971): 1–8.

"Where Pollution Control Is Slowing Industrial Growth." *U.S. News and World Report* 71 (August 23, 1971): 47–51.

Williams, Roger M. "TVA and the Strippers." *World* 2 (June 19, 1973): 20–25, 41.

Wood, T. D. "Audit Program for Compliance with Pollution Control Laws." *The CPA Journal* 44 (April 1974): 63–66.

Government Regulation and Law

Books

Georgescu-Roeger, Nicholas. *The Entropy Law and the Economic Process.* Cambridge, Mass: Harvard U. Press, 1971.

Hammaker, Paul M., ed. *The Pension Reform Law of 1974: Impact on American Society.* Center for the study of Applied Ethics, The Colgate Darden Graduate School of Business Administration, The University of Virginia, 1975.
> Proceedings from a conference on the Employee Retirement Income Security Act of 1974. This volume contains a thorough discussion of the legal, social, ethical and economic dimensions of the issue.

Jacoby, Neil. *The Business-Government Relationship: A Reassessment.* Pacific Palisades, Calif: Goodyear, 1975.

Kintner, Earl W. *An Antitrust Primer; A Guide to Antitrust and Trade Regulation Laws for Businessmen.* 2nd edition. New York: Macmillan, 1973.

Posner, Richard A. *Regulation of Advertising by the FTC.* Washington: American Enterprise Institute for Public Policy Research, 1973.

Stridsberg, A. B. *Effective Advertising Self-regulation.* New York: International Advertising Association, 1974.

Tindall, Robert Emmett. *Multinational Enterprises: Legal and Management Structures and Interrelationship with Ownership, Control, Antitrust, Labor, Taxation and Disclosure.* Dobbs Ferry, New York: Oceana Publications, Inc., 1975.

VanCise, Jerrold and Marcus Mattson, chairmen. *The New FTC Approach to Advertising Regulation.* New York: Practicing Law Institute, 1971.

Weilbacher, William M. *Marketing Management Cases,* second edition. New York: Macmillan Publishing Company, Inc., 1975.
    A part of this book deals with marketing tactics & issues of government regulations and social responsibility.

Williamson, Oliver. *Markets and Hierarchies: Analysis and Antitrust Implications·* New York: The Free Press, 1975.

Articles

Blair, Roger D. "Reciprocity and Competition: A Problem of Conflicting 'Assumptions.'" *Antitrust Law and Economics Review* 6 (1973): 77–86.

Casey, Wiliam J. "Corporate Responsibility as Seen from the SEC." *Business and Society Review* (Spring 1972): 24–28.

Chatov, Robert. "Independent Regulatory Agency Behavior." Mimeographed paper, 1972.

Cohen, Dorothy. "Concept of Unfairness As It Relates to Advertising Legislation." *Journal of Marketing* 38 (July 1974): 8–13.

Cohen, Manuel F. and George J. Stigler. "Can Regulatory Agencies Protect Consumers?" American Enterprise Institute. Rational debate Seminars Series 5, #4, 1971.

"Companies Tell More, Mostly to the SEC." *Business Week* (October 30, 1971): 26.

"Corrective Advertising Orders of the Federal Trade Commission." *Harvard Law Review* 85 (December 1971): 477–506.

Cramton, R. C. "Reflections on Law, Morality and Equal Justice." *Trusts and Estates* 114 (April 1975): 210–212+.

Davis, Rex D. "False Advertising: The Expanding Presence of the FTC." *Baylor Law Review* 25 (Fall 1973): 650–659.

Diggins, E. P. "Put on Your Overcoat: SEC Announces Phase 1 of Disclosing Corporate Prospects." *Public Relations Journal* 28 (October 1972): 16–19.

"Ethical Drug Ads Would Be Curbed Under FDA Rule." *Chemical Marketing Reporter* 202 (August 28, 1972): 4+.

Farris, Martin T. "Purchasing Reciprocity and Antitrust." *Journal of Purchasing* 9 (February 1973): 5–14.

"Federal Agencies Under Fire." *U.S. News and World Report* 69 (November 9, 1970): 82–84.

Ferguson, John R. and others. "Consumer Ignorance as a Source of Monopoly Power." *Antitrust Law and Economics Review* 5 (Winter 1971/72, Spring 1972): 79–102, 55–74.

"The FTC Ad Substantiation Program." *Georgetown Law Journal* 61 (July 1973): 1427–1452.

Gillis, J. G. "Legal Consequences of Unethical Conduct." *Financial Analysts Journal* 29 (November 1973): 12+.

Gossett, William T. "The Corporation Lawyer's Social Responsibilities." *American Bar Association Journal* 60 (December 1974): 1517–1520.

Graf, E. L., Jr. "Product Publicity and the Law." *Public Relations Journal* 27 (July 1971): 19–20+.

"ITT Continental Hit in Many Ways by FTC." *Broadcasting* 80 (March 22, 1971): 59.

129

Levenson, Alan B. "The Role of the SEC as a Consumer Protection Agency." *Business Lawyer* 27 (November 1971): 61–70.

Loevinger, Lee. "The Closed Mind Inquiry—Antitrust Report Is Raiders' Nadir." *Antitrust Bulletin* 17 (Fall 1972): 737–762.

Loevinger, Lee. "The Morality of Mergers: The Antitrust Trip from Economics to Ecclesiastes and Back." *Mergers and Acquisitions* 10 (Spring 1975): 16–30.

McCaffrey, James J. "Advertising and the Federal Trade Commission: A Reposte." *Journal of Advertising* 2 (November 1, 1973): 16–19.

Myers, John G. "Legislative Controls and Freedom of Speech: The Case of Commercial Advertising." *Public Affairs Report* 13 (August 1972): 1–5.

"New FTC: So Good It Hurts." *Sales Management; The Marketing Magazine* 106 (January 15, 1971): 30+.

"A New Plan for Regulating Industry." *U.S. News and World Report* 70 (February 22, 1971): 44–45.

Rodgers, William. "IBM on Trial." *Harper's* 248 (May 1974): 79–84.
    One of the largest multinational business corporations on trial for becoming too powerful and ruthless and not allowing competitors a chance.

Rogers, William D. "Antitrust: How Far Does the Writ Run?" *Columbia Journal of World Business* 6 (March/April 1971): 46–50.
    The integrity of competition in world business is jeopardized by nationalistic antitrust competition.

Rome, Edwin P. "Antitrust Problems in Multinational Corporations." *Conference Board Record* 9 (August 1972): 55–58.

Schuck, Peter H. "Why Regulation Fails." *Ha.   's* 251 (September 1975): 16–29.
    Federal regulatory agencies harm both public and private interest.

Tarpey, L. X. "Buyer Liability Under the Robinson—Patman Act: A Current Appraisal." *Journal of Marketir* 36 (January 1972): 38–42.

"Using Antitrust for Civil Rights." *Business Wee.* (December 8, 1973): 62.

Werther, William B. Jr. "Government Control vs. Corporate Ingenuity." *Labor Law Journal* (June 1975): 360+.

Wiedenbaum, Murray L. "The High Cost of Government Regulation." *Business Horizons* 18 (August 1975): 43–51.

Wilson, James J. "The Dead Hand of Regulation." *The Public Interest* 25 (Fall 1971): 39–58.
    Discusses the problems of federal regulation to act in best public interest, especially in the matters of efficiency and equity.

Investment Policy and Shareholder Responsibility

Books

Annual Report—1975, Interfaith Center on Corporate Responsibility. New York: The Corporate Information Center, 1975.
    Other reports and materials are available from this center.

Directory of the National Catholic Coalition for Responsible Investment. Milwaukee, Wisconsin: National Catholic Coalition for Responsible Investment, 1975.
    A booklet containing a history of the corporate responsibility movement.

Investor Relations: The Information Explosion. Washington: National Investor Relations Institute, 1971.
    Proceedings of the First Annual National Conference, Washington, D.C., 1970.

Investor Relations, 1972: *Challenge & Response.* Washington: National Investor Relations Institute, 1971.
    Proceedings of Second Annual National Conference, Washington, D.C., 1971 with some discussion of industry and social aspects.

General Electric Company, *General Electric Investor.* New York: General Electric Company, 1973.

Longotreth, Bevis and H. David Rosenbloom. *Corporate Social Responsibility and the Institutional Investor: A Report to the Ford Foundation.* New York: Praeger Publishers, Inc., 1973.
    A well documented study covering all relevant aspects of the issue.

Powers, Charles W., ed. *People Profits: The Ethics of Investments.* New York: Council on Religion and International Affairs, 1972.

A representative selection of papers and edited responses on the issue of social investment with both theoretical and practical dimensions discussed.

Powers, Charles W. *Social Responsibility and Investments.* Nashville: Abingdon Press, 1971.

Simon, John G., Charles Powers and Jon P. Gunneman. *The Ethical Investor: Universities and Corporate Responsibility.* New Haven, Connecticut: Yale University Press, 1972.

Articles

"American Bankers Association Issues Social Responsibility Guidelines for Trust Investments [Southern Trust Conference]." *Trusts and Estates* 112 (August 1973): 548+.

Ayres, R. M., Jr. "Investment Bankers Must Take Active Role in Solving All of the Nation's Problems." *Commercial and Financial Chronicle* 213 (April 8, 1971): 1080–1081.

Baker, James C., et al. "Institutional Investor Attitudes Toward Corporate Social Responsibility." *Arkansas Business & Economic Review* 7 (Summer 1974): 14–20.

Brown, S. "Citibank's Fiduciary Accounts Gain 23%—Reporting Breaks with Tradition by Including Corporate Responsibility in Investment Criteria." *Commercial and Financial Chronicle* 215 (March 23, 1972): 958.

Casey, William J. "Corporate Responsibility as Seen from the SEC." *Business and Society Review* 1 (Spring 1972): 24–28.

The head of the Securities and Exchange Commission views proxy rules, shareholder proposals, and disclosure policies as tools to implement corporate accountability.

Charles, George. "What Investors Think About 'Social' Investing." *Business and Society Review* 14 (Summer 1975): 74–78.

Cross, Theodore and Paul London. "It Makes a Difference Where You Bank Your Money." *Business and Society Review/Innovation* 8 (Winter 1973–74): 22–31.

Personal banking with a sense of social responsibility. Data is provided on banks in New York City for purposes of consumer shopping.

Eastburn, David P. "The Securities Business and Consciousness III." *Federal Reserve Philadelphia* (January 1971): 3–7.

Hall, J. Parker III. "Professional Investors' View of Social Responsibility." *Financial Analysts Journal* 27 (September/October 1971): 32–34.

Healy, Gerald W. "The Stockholder and the Morality in the Angry Seventies." *World Justice* 12 (December 1970): 167–198.

Hoy, James B. "Socal's Dissident Shareholders Mobilize." *Business and Society Review* (Winter 1975–76): 42–48.
An account of how "Project Standard Oil" was started and a report of some shareholder activities.

"Institutions That Balk at Anti-Social Management." *Business Week* (January 19, 1974): 66–67.
A discussion of how proxies are being used to change management decisions and policies.

"Investment in Corporations or Projects Designed Primarily to Promote Community Welfare." *Federal Reserve Bulletin* 58 (June 1972): 572.

Jacquette, F. Lee. "Public Interest Investment by Banks." *Bankers Magazine* 157 (Autumn 1974): 115–122.

Longotreth, Bevis. "Social Aspects of Business Behavior—Issue for Institutional Investors." *Trusts and Estates* 112 (May 1973): 322–325+.

Malkiel, Burton G. and Richard E. Quandt. "Moral Issues in Investment Policy." *Harvard Business Review* 49 (March/April 1971): 37–47.

Manne, Henry G. "Shareholder Social Proposals Viewed by an Opponent." *Stanford Law Review* 24 (February 1972): 481–506.

"Moral Power of Shareholders." *Business Week* (May 1, 1971): 76+.

Moskowitz, Milton. "Choosing Socially Responsible Stocks." *Business and Society Review* 1 (Spring 1972): 71–75.

"The Movement for Corporate Responsibility." *Economic Priorities Report* 2 (April/May 1971): 1+.
Concerning efforts of some shareholders to influence individual corporate social performance.

"New Proxy Warfare." *Nation's Business* 59 (August 1971): 58–63.

Preston, Ronald. "Ethics of Investment." *Theology* 78 (October 1975): 507–518.

Schwartz, Donald E. "The 1972 Annual Meetings: An Active Season but Signs of Decline." *Business and Society Review* (Autumn 1972): 54–59.
Proxy contests are a cheap way for social activities to publicize their causes. Does it matter that they always lose?

Schwartz, Donald E. "The Public Interest Proxy Contest: Reflections on Campaign GM." 3 *Michigan Law Review* 69 (1971).

Schwartz, Robert. "A Cold Eye on Guilt-edged Investing." *Business and Society Review* 3 (Autumn 1972): 81+.
Clean investments are really possible according to the author.

Shapiro, Harvey D. "Social Responsibility Funds Get Off to a Bad Start." *Business and Society Review/Innovation,* Volume 11 (Spring 1973): 81–87.

Shapiro, Harvey D. "Social Responsibility Mutual Funds." *Business and Society Review* 12 (Winter 1974–75): 90–93.

"Shareholder Activism." *Economic Priorities Report* 5 (November 3, 1974): 59–63.

Slaven, Peter. "They Do Homework for Big Investors." *Business and Society Review/Innovation* 8 (Winter 1973–74): 50–51.
A profile of the Investor Responsibility Research Center, a small nonprofit organization in Washington, D.C.

"Social Activists Stir Up the Annual Meeting." *Business Week* (April 1, 1972): 48–49.

Stabler, Charles and Barry Newman. "Speaking Out." *Wall Street Journal* 177 (April 28, 1971): 1+.

Minorities

Books

Basil, Douglas C. *Women in Management: Performance, Prejudice, Promotion.* Port Washington, N.Y.: Dunellen Publishing Company, 1972.

Becker, Gary S. *Economics of Discrimination.* Revised 2nd edition. Chicago: University of Chicago Press, 1971.

Bird, Caroline. *What Every Woman Needs to Know to Get Paid What She's Worth.* New York: McKay, 1973.

Blumrosen, Alfred W. *Black Employment & the Law.* New Brunswick, New Jersey: Rutgers University Printers, 1971.

Bramwell, Jonathan. *Courage in Crisis: The Black Professional Today.* Indianapolis, Indiana. Bobbs-Merrill, 1973.

Brown, James K. and Seymour Lusterman. *Business and the Development of Ghetto Enterprise.* New York: National Industrial Conference Board, 1971.

Calvert, Robert, Jr. Equal *Employment Opportunity for Minority Group College Graduates: Locating, Recruiting, Employing.* Garrett Park, Maryland: Garrett Park Press, 1972.

Campbell, Helen. *Women Wage-Earners: Their Past, Their Present, & Their Future.* (American Women Series: Images & Realities). New York: Arno, 1972.

Case, Frederick E. *Inner City Housing and Private Enterprise.* New York: Praeger, 1972.

Cash, William L., Jr. and Lucy R. Oliver, eds. *Black Economic Development: Analysis & Implications.* Ann Arbor, Michigan: University of Michigan Business Research, 1975.

Coleman, James S. *Resources in Social Change: Race in the United States.* (Urban Research Series). New York: Wiley-Interscience, 1971.

Coles, Flournoy A., Jr. *Black Economic Development.* Chicago, Illinois: Nelson-Hall, 1975.

Cross, Theodore L. *Black Capitalism: Strategy for Business in the Ghetto*. New York: Atheneum, 1971.

Darling, Martha. *The Role of Women in the Economy*. OCED Publications Center, Suite 1207, 1750 Pennsylvania Avenue, N.W., Washington, D.C. 20006.
   A report on the amount and scope of participation of women in the labor force.

Dennis, Lloyd V. *Community Performance: An Action Report of California Bankers*. San Francisco: California Bankers Association, 1973.

Feldman, Herman. *Racial Factors in American Industry*. New York: Ozer, 1971.

Fernandez, John P. *Black Managers in White Corporations*. New York: Wiley-Interscience, 1975.

Gelber, Steven M. *Black Men & Businessman: The Growing Awareness of a Social Responsibility*. Port Washington, New York: Kennikat, 1974.

Gelber, Steven M. *Business Values & Black Employment: A Case Study in Cultural Adaptation*. Menlo Park, California: Cummings, 1973.

Ginzberg, Eli, ed. *Corporate Lib: Women's Challenge to Management*. (Policy Studies in Employment & Welfare, PSEW 17). Baltimore, Maryland: Johns Hopkins, 1973.

Hampton, David and Edwin Epstein. *Black Americans & White Business*. Belmont, California: Dickenson, 1971.

Harbeson, Gladys. *Choice & Challenge for the American Woman.* 2nd ed. Cambridge, Massachusetts: Schenkman, 1972.

Irons, Edward D. *On Black Economic Development: Myths & Facts*. Austin, Texas: University of Texas Business Research, 1971.

Janger, Allen R. *Employing the Disadvantaged: A Company Perspective*. New York: National Industrial Conference Board, 1972.

Jones, Edward H. *Blacks in Business*. New York: Grossett & Dunlap, 1971.

Killian, Ray A. *The Working Woman: A Male Manager's View*. New York: American Management Associations, 1971.

Kreps, Juanita. *Sex in the Marketplace: American Women at Work.* Baltimore, Maryland: Johns Hopkins, 1971.

Lacy, Dan. *White Use of Blacks in America.* New York: Atheneum, 1972.

Light, Ivan H. *Ethnic Enterprise in America: Business & Welfare Among Chinese, Japanese, & Blacks.* Berkeley, California: University of California Printing, 1973.

Loring, Rosalind & Theodora Wells. *Breakthrough: Women into Management.* New York: Van Nos Reinhold, 1972.

Lyle, Jerolyn R. & Jane Ross. *Women in Industry.* Lexington, Massachusetts: Lexington Books, 1973.

MacEachen, Allen J. *Profiles of Involvement,* Vol. I, II, III. Philadelphia, Pa.: Human Resources Corporation, 1972.
    Include considerable data on business involvement in minority and urban problems.

Madden, Janice F. *The Economics of Sex Discrimination.* Lexington, Massachusetts: Lexington Books, 1973.

Martin, Claude R. *Support for Women's Lib: Management Performance.* Ann Arbor, Michigan: Bureau of Business Research, University of Michigan, 1971.
    This book deals with purchasing agents, discrimination in employment and employment of women in particular.

Mestre, Eloy. *Economic Minorities in Manpower Development.* Lexington, Massachussetts: Lexington Books, 1972.

Murphy, Irene L. *Public Policy on the Status of Women.* Lexington, Massachusetts: Lexington Books, 1973.

Office of Minority Business Enterprise. *Progress Report: The Minority Business Enterprise Program, 1972.* Washington, D.C.: U.S. Department of Commerce, October 1972.

Office of Minority Business Enterprise. *Special Catalog of Federal Programs Assisting Minority Enterprise.* Washington, D.C.: U.S. Department of Commerce, Summer 1971.

O'Neil, F. Hodge. *Oppression of Minority Shareholders.* Callaghan & Company, 6141 North Cicero Avenue, Chicago, Illinois, 1975.

137

This book is addressed to accountants and legal specialists. Squeeze out techniques are treated in depth.

Pressley, Milton M. *A Selected Bibliography of Readings and References Regarding Marketing to Black Americans.* Greensboro, North Carolina: Council of Planning Librarians, 1974.

Pruette, Lorine. *Women & Leisure: A Study of Social Waste.* (American Women Series: Images & Realities). New York: Arno, 1972.

Purcell, Theodore and Gerald Cavanagh. *Blacks in the Industrial World: Issues for the Manager.* New York: The Free Press, 1972. Written from the perspective of ethics.

Puryear, Alvin N. and Charles A. West. *Black Enterprise, Incorporated.* New York: Doubleday, 1973.

Ruchames, Louis. *Race, Jobs & Politics: The Story of the FEPC.* Westport, Connecticut: Negro Universities Press, 1972.

Seder, John and Berkeley G. Burrell. *Getting It Together: Black Businessmen in America.* New York: Harcourt Brace Jovanovich, 1971.

Shaeffer, Ruth G. *Nondiscrimination in Employment: A Broadening and Deepening National Effort.* The Conference Board, Inc. 677, New York, New York, July 1975.
A thorough investigation of EEO practices in firms from 1972–1975.

Shaeffer, Ruth G. *Nondiscrimination in Employment: Changing Perspectives, 1963–1972.* New York: National Industrial Conference Board, 1973.

Simmons, Adele et al. *Exploitation from Nine to Five: Report of the Twentieth Century Fund Task Force on Women & Employment Background.* Lexington, Massachusetts: Lexington Books, 1975.

Strober, Myra H. *Bringing Women into Management.* New York: McGraw-Hill Book Company, 1975.

Taylor, Vernon R. *Employment of the Disadvantaged in the Public Service.* Chicago, Illinois: International Personnel Management, 1971.

Tsuchigane, Robert. *Discrimination Against Women in the U.S. Economy.* Lexington, Massachusetts: Lexington Books, 1974.

138

Tsuchigane, Robert and Norton T. Dodge. *Economic Discrimination Against Women in the U.S.* Lexington, Massachusetts: Lexington Books, 1974.

Turgeon, Lynn. *The Economics of Discrimination.* (Studies on Developing Countries, No. 62). New York: International Publishers Service, 1974.

Venable, Abraham S. *Building Black Business: An Analysis and A Plan.* New York: Earl G. Graves Publishing Company, 1972.

Weare, Walter B. *Black Business in the New South: A Social History of the North Carolina Mutual Life Insurance Company.* Urbana, Illinois: University of Illinois Press, 1973.

Women in Business. New York: American Management Association, 1973.

Zimpel, Lloyd. *Disadvantaged Worker: Readings in Developing Minority Manpower.* Reading, Massachusetts: Addison-Wesley, 1971.

Articles

Ace, M. E. "Psychological Testing: Unfair Discrimination?" *Industrial Relations* 10 (October 1971): 301–315.

Alexander, Don H. "The Black Businessman—Hope for the Future." *University of Washington Business Review* 30 (Winter 1971): 15–20.

Allan, V. R. "Matter of Simple Justice." *SAM Advanced Management Journal* 36 (October 1971): 49–52.

Allsop, Thomas. "Boston and Prudential Center." *Journal of Contemporary Business* (Spring 1974): 89–102.
    An awakened social consciousness in Prudential. Interesting report.

"American Industry Finding the Formula to Help Minorities." *Commerce Today* 2 (May 1, 1972): 12–16.

"Anti-Discrimination; Committee Points." *Economist* 246 (March 3, 1973): 19–20.

"Barbs That Hurt Businesswomen." *Business Week* (February 19, 1972): 50+.

Bender, Marilyn. "Women at Avon: No Room at the Top." *Business and Society Review/Innovation* 4 (Winter 1972–73): 19–24.

Bittker, Boris. "The Case for Black Reparations." *Business and Society Review/Innovation* 5 (Spring 1973): 48–54.

"Black and the Green." *Forbes* 110 (September 15, 1972): 45–48.

"The Black Message: Business Must Do More." *Business Week* (January 22, 1972): 79–80.
  Top businessmen believe blacks have made real economic progress, but black leaders insist more help on jobs and pay is needed.

"Blacks in Business." Master in Business Administration (February 1971).
  The whole issue is devoted to subject.

Blumrosen, Alfred W. "Removing Roadblocks to Minority Hiring." *Monthly Labor Review* 95 (April 1972): 23–24.
  The failure to curb racial discrimination in hiring casts doubt on the ability of the Federal Government to provide for basic civil rights.

Boyle, M. Barbara. "Equal Opportunity for Women Is Smart Business." *Harvard Business Review* 51 (May 1973): 85–95.
  It is smart because this largest minority (40% of the work force) is an almost untapped resource of talent and skills.

Brothers, Joyce. "Are You a Male Chauvinist Boss?" *Supervisory Management* 17 (December 1972): 2–8.

Brown, James K. and Seymour Lusterman. "Business and the Development of Ghetto Enterprise." *Conference Board Report* 517 (1971): IV + 105p.

"Business Efforts to Aid in Ghetto Missing Goals." *Industry Week* 169 (May 17, 1971): 11–12.

Carson, L. "Black Director—Mostly Black, or Mostly Director?" *Management Review* 62 (December 1973): 50–52.

Case, Frederick E. "Housing the Underhoused in the Inner City." *The Journal of Finance* (May 1971).

Cass, James. "Minority Rights in a Democratic Society." *Saturday Review* (January 15, 1972): 51.

Chambers, Peter. "No Easy Path for Women Managers." *International Management* 2 (May 1974): 46–98.

Chapman, Jane Roberts. "Women's Access to Credit." *Challenge* 17 (January/February 1975): 40–45.

Clark P. "Sexism and the Secretary." *Dun's* 99 (January 1972): 69/70.

"Combating Sex Discrimination in the United States." *International Labour Review* 106 (August-September 1972): 269/273.

"Corporation Leaders Respond with Action on Minority Effort." *Commerce Today* 3 (October 1, 1973): 8–11.

Cross, Theodore. "Closing Down Markets for Discrimination." *Business and Society Review/Innovation* 4 (Winter 1972-73): 25.

Crotty, Philip T. and Jeffry A. Timmons. "Older Minorities—Road-blocked in the Organization." *Business Horizons* 17 (June 1974): 27–34.

Crowle Vivian and Barbara B. Carroll. "How to Deal Women into the Game." *Industry Week* 176 (January 15, 1973): 31–36.
Affirmative action can be a long-term profitable assessment of human resources.

Davis, Earl F., Warren A. French, and Rudolph L. Kagerer. "Establishment of a Minority Small Business Training Program: In Retrospect." *MSU Business Topics* 21 (Spring 1973): 64–72.
This disheartening case study shows how a good idea was not enough; operational goals, leadership, planning and control were lacking.

Domm, Donald R. and James E. Stafford. "Assimilating Blacks into the Organization." *California Management Review* 15 (Fall 1972): 46–51.

Edwards, H. T. "Sex Discrimination Under Title VII: Some Unresolved Issues." *Labor Law Journal* 24 (July 1973): 411–423.

Engeman, W. K. "Fair Employment Practices." *Labor Law Journal* 22 (August 1971): 513–538.

"Free the Women?" *Industry Week* 170 (July 26, 1971): 34–42.

Gerry, Gloria J. "Hiring Minorities and Women: The Selection Process." *Personnel Journal* 53 (December 1974): 906–909.
The essay argues that selection standards ought to be revised in order to lessen the chance of discrimination.

Gillooly, Thomas J. "Equal Rights and Insurance." *Chartered Life Underwriters* 29 (January 1975): 37–41.
Effects of sex discrimination on life and health insurance.

Goldman, Alan. "Affirmative Action." *Philosophy and Public Affairs* 5 (Winter 1976): 178–195.
Reverse discrimination may be a justified form of compensation for certain individuals, but is not justified in the form encouraged by numerical goals.

Graves, Earl G. "Eliminating Discrimination Can Increase Productivity." *The Personnel Administrator* 20 (June 1975): 50–52.
The role of the black American in increasing productivity has been largely ignored, according to the author.

Hackamack, Lawrence C. and Alan B. Solid. "Woman Executive." *Business Horizons* 15 (April 1972): 89–93.

Hecht, James L. "Employers Join to Promote Open Housing." *Harvard Business Review* 51 (July 1973): 14, 150–152.

Hills, Gerald E. and Gerald E. Nichols. "Business and the Minority Community." *Tennessee Survey of Business* 7 (May 1972): 3–6+.

Hogan, Patricia. "A Woman Is Not a Girl and Other Lessons in Corporate Speech." *Business and Society Review* 14 (Summer 1975): 34–38.
A discussion of sexist language in corporations.

Holsendolph, Ernest. "Black Executives in a Nearly All-White World." *Fortune* 86 (September 1972): 140–144+.
An interesting article on the possibilities and hazards of climbing to the top.

Hyatt, James C. "No-account Females." *Wall Street Journal* 180 (July 18, 1972): 1+.

Jackson, Charles W. "Operation Incentive: A Motivation Program." *Business Horizons* 15 (December 1972): 85–88.

A company has a unique method of upgrading minority employees called Operation Incentive.

Jacobson, Carolyn J. "ERA: Ratifying Equality." *American Federationist* 82 (January 1975): 9–13.

Jones, Edward W., Jr. "What It's Like to Be a Black Manager." *Harvard Business Review* 51 (July 1973): 108–116.

Joseph, James A. "Corporate Philanthropy and Community Development: The Cummins Engine Company's Approach." *Journal of Contemporary Business* (Spring 1974): 79–88.
Cummins' well known and long-standing commitment to an equalitarian society led to the development of social and economic programs to help the plight of minorities. An illuminating report.

"Key to Minority Hiring: Total Involvement." *Chemical Week* 116 (March 26, 1975): 18–19.

Kitchings, Suzanne Donnelly. "EEOC Regulatory Intervention." *Georgetown Law Review* 62 (July 1974): 1753–1770.

Klein, Richard H. "A Perspective on the MESBIC Program." *MSU Business Topics* 20 (Autumn 1972): 45–51.
Reasonable profitability in the long run "may be illusory" despite proposed changes and modifications in procedure. MESBIC = Minority Enterprise Small Business Investment Company.

Kristol, Irving. "About Equality." *Commentary* 54, 5 (November 1972): 41–47.

Ledvinka, James and William W. Pearson. "On Developing New Minority Businessmen." *Journal of Small Business Management* (January 1971): 26–30.

McGuire, Joseph W. and John R. Parrish. "States Report on a Profound Revolution." *California Management Review* 13 (Summer 1971).
Statistics on business social involvement in the cities.

McKelvey, J. T. "Sex and the Single Arbitrator." *Industrial & Labor Relations Review* 24 (April 1971): 335–353.

"Minority Entrepreneurship: Special Report on a Seminar." *Atlanta Economic Review* 21 (February 1971): 12–30.

Moore, John M. "Transferring Minority Employees: Are They Being Treated Fairly?" *Personnel Journal* 54 (February 1975): 84, 85, 125.

Discrimination in certain communities is discussed as an ethical and practical problem for business.

Moskowitz, Milton. "The Black Directors: Tokenism or a Big Leap Forward?" *Business and Society Review* 3 (Autumn 1972): 73–80.

The number of black directors appointed to major boards has increased tenfold in the last two years. He is a thorough report on who they are and where they are.

Myrdal, Gunner. "The Relentless Drive Toward Equalitarianism." *Business and Society Review/Innovation* 7 (Autumn 1973): 14–19.

Nason, Robert W. "Dilemma of Black Mobility in Management." *Business Horizons* 15 (August 1972): 57–68.

O'Brien, Conor Cruise. "On the Rights of Minorities." *Commentary* 55, 56 (June 1973): 46–50.

Ornati, Oscar A. and Edward Giblin. "The High Cost of Discrimination." *Business Horizons* 18 (February 1975): 35–40.

Petersen, Gary G. and Linda Bryant. "Eliminating Sex Discrimination—Who Must Act?" *Personnel Journal* 51 (August 1972): 587–591.

Purcell, Theodore V. "The Case of the Borderline Black." *Harvard Business Review* (November-December): 128–133, 142–150.

"Recession Clashes With Race Question." *Broadcasting* 80 (February 8, 1971): 30.

Reif, W. E. and Others. "Exploding Some Myths about Women Managers." *California Management Review* 17 (Summer 1975): 72–79.

Rhine, Shirley H. "The Economic Status of Black Americans." *The Conference Board Record* (August 1972).

Because of change some of the historical differences have been lessened.

Robertson, David E. "Employment Testing and Discrimination." *Personnel Journal* 54 (January 1975): 18–21, 56.

An emphasis is put on consistency and clarity in establishing and implimenting testing guidelines. Discrimination is defined.

144

Roeser, Thomas F. "The Quaker Oats Company and Urban Affairs." *Journal of Contemporary Business* (Spring 1974): 103–109.
A report on projects carried out by Quaker that aimed at social benefit.

Rosen, Benson and Thomas H. Jerdee. "Sex Stereotyping in the Executive Suite." *Harvard Business Review* 52 (March 1974): 45–58.

Schwartz, Eleanor B. and James J. Rago, Jr. "Beyond Tokenism: Women as True Corporate Peers." *Business Horizons* 16 (December 1973): 69–76.
The authors explore the phenomenon of male executive resistance to working with women as peers.

Schwartz, Felice. "Converging Work Roles of Men and Women." *Business and Society Review/Innovation* 7 (Autumn 1973): 71–75.

Shepherd, W. G. and S. G. Levin. "Managerial Discrimination in Large Firms." *Review of Economics & Statistics* 55 (November 1973): 412–422.

Short, Larry E. "Nondiscrimination Policies: Are They Effective?" *Personnel Journal* 52 (September 1973): 786–792.
The author argues that EEOA will result in the employment of more minorities but will not accomplish equality of opportunity.

Slevin, D. P. "What Companies Are Doing About Women's Job Equality." *Personnel* 48 (July 1971): 8–18.

"Social Action Survives If It's Good Business." *Industry Week* 169 (June 14, 1971):

"Social Issues, Expertise Worry Minority Builders." *Engineering News Record* 188 (April 20, 1972): 61.

Stead, B. A. "Real Equal Opportunity for Women Executives." *Business Horizons* 17 (August 1974): 87–92.

Steiner, George. "Business and Disadvantaged Minorities in the Cities." *Journal of Contemporary Business* (Spring 1974): 29–60.
An evaluation of the problems and guideline proposals.

Stone, M. L. "There's No Accounting for Women." *The CPA Journal* 42 (October 1972): 802–803.

Stull, Richard Allen. "New Answers to an Old Question: Woman's Place Is in the What?" *Personnel Journal* 52 (January 1973): 31–35.

"U.S. Firms Take Lead in Helping Minorities." *Commerce Today* 1 (March 22, 1971): 14–17.

Vance, Stanley C. "Black Power in the Board Room: Token or Reality?" *Business Horizons* 14 (June 1971): 81–88.

Verway, David I. "Advance to the Rear for Women." *MSU Business Topics* 20 (Winter 1972): 53–62.

"What Economic Equality for Women Requires." *American Economic Review* 62 (May 1972): 157–176.

"Who Are the Women in the Board Rooms?" *Business and Society Review* 16 (Winter 1975–76): 5–10.
    This *Business and Society* review is the first comprehensive list of women board members to be published.

"Women and Minorities in Management." *Monthly Labor Review* 95 (March 1972): 55.

"Women Now Want Credit Liberated." *Business Week* (May 6, 1972): 36+.

"Women Seek Equal Chances in Business." *Commerce Today* 2 (July 10, 1972): 4–7.

Woods, Marion M. "What Does It Take for a Woman to Make It in Management." *Personnel Journal* 54 (January 1975): 38–41, **66**.

"You Still Have a Long Way to Go—Baby." *Business Week* (September 25, 1971): 74–76.

Multinational Corporations and Social Issues

Books

Aitken, Thomas. *The Multinational Man: The Role of the Manager Abroad*. New York: Wiley, 1973.

Bagley, Edward R. *Beyond the Conglomerates—The Impact of the Supercorporation on the Future of Life and Business*. New York: American Management Associations, 1975.
    Analyzes the impact of supercorporations on business and society.

146

Barnet, Richard J. and Ronald E. Muller. *Global Reach: The Power of the Multinational Corporations.* New York: Simon and Schuster, 1971.

A scathing analysis of the power and pretensions of multinationals written in a popular literary style and undergirded with thorough research. A blockbuster book.

Behrman, Jack N. *Conflicting Constraints on the Multinational Enterprise: Potential for Resolution.* New York: Council of the Americas, 1974.

Beter, Peter. *The Conspiracy Against the Dollar: The Spirit of the New Imperialism.* New York: G. Braziller, 1973.

Blake, David H., ed. *The Multinational Corporation.* Philadelphia: American Academy of Political and Social Science, 1972.

Boarman, Patrick M. and Hans Schollhammer. *Multinational Corporations and Governments.* New York: Praeger, 1975.

Based on proceedings of a conference held in late 1973 at UCLA.

Brooke, Michael Zachary and H. L. Remmers, eds. *The Multinational Company in Europe: Some Key Problems.* Ann Arbor, Michigan: University of Michigan Press, 1974.

Cateora, Philip R. and John M. Hess. *International Marketing.* Homewood, Illinois: R. D. Irwin, 1971.

Crystal, Graef S. *Conspensating U.S. Executives Abroad.* New York: American Management Association, 1972.

Dymoza, William A. *Multinational Business Strategy.* New York: McGraw Hill, 1971.

Eells, Richard. *Global Corporations.* New York: Interbook, 1972.

Fatimi, Nasrollah Saifpour and G. W. Williams. *Multinational Corporations: The Problems and Prospects.* Cranbury, N.J.: Fairleigh Dickenson University Press, 1975.

Feld, Warner J. *Nongovernmental Forces and World Politics: A Study of Business, Labor, and Political Groups.* New York: Praeger Publishers, 1972.

Franko, Lawrence G. *Joint Venture Survival in Multinational Corporations.* New York: Praeger Publishers, 1971.

147

Ganguli, Birendranath. *Multinational Corporations*. Mystic, Connecticut: Verry, 1974.

Gilpin, Robert. *The Multinational Corporation and the National Interest*. Washington: U. S. Government Printing Office, 1973.

Hays, Richard D., Christopher M. Korth and Manucher Roudiani. *International Business: An Introduction to the World of the Multinational Firm*. Englewood Cliffs, N.J.: Prentice-Hall, 1971.

Heenan, David A. *Multinational Management of Human Resources: A System Approach*. Austin Bureau of Business Research, University of Texas, 1975.

Hodges, Michael. *Multinational Corporations and National Government*. Washington, D.C.: American Office of Health, 1974.
A case study of United Kingdom's experience.

International Labor Office. *Multinational Enterprises and Social Policy*. Geneva: International Labor Office, 1973.

Jackson, Richard A. *The Multinational Corporation and Social Policy*. New York: Praeger, 1974.
This book contains the prepared papers and abridged discussion from a Council on Religious and International Affairs consultation. It includes an introduction by Charles Powers and gives special attention to General Motors in South Africa.

Jacoby, Neil. *Multinational Oil: A Study in Industrial Dynamics*. New York: Free Press, 1975.

Levinson, Charles. *Capital, Inflation, and the Multinationals*. New York: Macmillan, 1972.

Modelski, George, ed. *Multinational Corporations and World Order*. Beverly Hills, California: Sage Publications, 1972.

Moran, Theodore. *Multinational Corporations and the Politics of Dependence*. Princeton: Princeton University Press, 1975.
Written under the auspices of the Center for International Affairs, Harvard University, about copper in Chile.

Phatak, Arvind V. *Evolution of World Enterprises*. New York: American Management Association, 1971.

Phatak, Arvind V. *Managing Multinational Corporations*. New York: Praeger, 1974.

Plummer, Alfred. *International Combines in Modern Industry.* Freeport, New York: Books for Libraries Press, 1971.

Ricks, David A., Marilyn Y. C. Fu and Jeffrey S. Arpan, *International Business Blunders.* Columbus, Ohio: Grid, Incorporated, 1974.

Robock, Stefan H. and Kenneth Simmonds. *International Business and Multinational Enterprises.* Homewood, Illinois: R. D. Irwin, 1973.

Said, Abdul A. and Luiz R. Simmons, ed. *The New Sovereigns: Multinational Corporations as World Powers.* Englewood Cliff, New Jersey: Prentice Hall, Incorporated, 1975.

Sampson, Anthony. *The Seven Sisters: The Great Oil Companies & the World They Shaped.* New York: The Viking Press, 1975.
  The author emphasizes the human side of the oil story and the impact of that story on the social order.

Sampson, Anthony. *The Sovereign State of ITT.* New York: Stein & Day, 1973.

Scheer, Robert. *America After Nixon: The Age of the Multinations.* New York: McGraw-Hill, 1974.

Schwendiman, John Snow. *Strategic and Long-Range Planning for the Multinational Corporation.* New York: Praeger, 1973.
  This book defines key elements of international corporate planning and reports on the state of the art.

Sethi, S. Prakash and Jagdish N. Sheth. *Environmental Aspects of Operating Abroad.* Pacific Palisades, California: Goodyear Publishing Company, 1973.

Stopford, John M. and Louis T. Wells, Jr. *Managing the Multinational Enterprise.* New York: Basic Books, 1972.

Tugendhat, Christopher. *The Multinationals.* New York: Random House, 1972.

Turner, Louis. *Invisible Empires: Multinational Companies and the Modern World.* New York: Harcourt Brace Jovanovich, 1971.

United States Senate, Committee on Finance, Subcommittee on International Trade. *The Multinational Corporation and the World Economy.* Washington, D.C.: Superintendent of Documents, 1973.

Turner, Louis. *Multinational Companies and the Third World.* New York: Hill and Wang, 1973.

United States Senate, Committee on Finance, Subcommittee on International Trade. *Multinational Corporations: A Compendium of Papers.* Washington, D.C.: Superintendent of Documents, 1973.

United States Senate, Committee on Finance, Subcommittee on International Trade. *Multinational Corporations: Hearings, February 26-March 6, 1973.* Washington, D.C.: Superintendent of Documents, 1973.

Vernon, Raymond. *The Economic and Political Consequences of Multinational Enterprise: An Anthology.* Boston: Division of Research, Graduate School of Business Administration, Harvard University, 1972.

Vernon, Raymond. *Sovereignty at Bay; The Multinational Spread of U.S. Enterprises.* New York: Basic Books, 1971.

Wilkens, Mira. *The Maturing of Multinational Enterprise: American Business Abroad from 1914 to 1970.* Cambridge, Massachusetts: Harvard University Press, 1974.
A thorough chronological history emphasizing the interrelationships between national economic policies and priorities and a changing international economic order.

Articles

Ball, George W. "Citizenship and the Multinational Corporation." *Social Research* 41 (Winter 1974): 657–672.

Ball, George W. "Nationalism—The Old and Growing Threat to the Multinational Corporation." *Corporate Financing* 4 (January/February 1972): 27–33+.

Barnet, Richard J. "Interview: Richard Barnet on Multinational Corporations." *Sojourners* 5 (February 1976): 14–19.

Bauer, D. "Indefinitely Defined Multinational." *Conference Board Record* 12 (July 1975): 21–24.

Behrman, Jack N. "Can Governments Slay the Dragons of Multinational Enterprise?" *European Business* (Winter 1971): 53–60.

Behrman, Jack N. "Is There a Better Way for Latin America?" *Columbia Journal of World Business* 6 (November/December 1971): 61–

71.

Discusses how the multinational corporation might be used effectively to accelerate industrial integration within Latin America and between that region and the advanced countries.

Behrman, Jack N. "The Multinational Enterprise and Economic Internationalism." *World Development* 3 (November/December 1975): 845–856.

Discusses the question of whether multinational enterprises, which have been praised as means of achieving the most efficient use of the world's resources and as a new means to classical economic internationalism, are likely to contribute to this goal.

Benoit, Emile. "The Attack on the Multinationals." *Columbia Journal of World Business* 7 (November 1972): 15–22.

The author asserts that if the United States multinational corporations are to survive, some obvious misconceptions on the part of their critics must be dispelled.

Bradley, Gene E. and Edward C. Bursk. "Multinationalism and the 29th Day." *Harvard Business Review* 50 (January/February 1972): 37–47.

Interviews with two top executives define the obstacles, the opportunities, facing global corporations in the years ahead. Topics of discussion include nationalism, centralized versus decentralized authority, market orientation and social responsibility.

"Brazil Has Second Thoughts About Multinationals: But Open Door Policy Remains for Now." *Multinational Business* (September 1975): 18–27.

Breckenfeld, Gurney. "Coping with the Nation-State." *Saturday Review* (January 24, 1976): 12–22.

Multinational corporations are subject to corruption and need regulation and control.

"Bribery, Corruption, or Necessary Fees and Charges?" *Multinational Business* (September 1975): 1–17.

A discussion of the ethical aspects of United States multinationals' use of political contributions and payment of "agents' or consultants' " fees as a means of promoting foreign business or obtaining special favors.

Brundenius, Claes. "The Anatomy of Imperialism: The Case of the Multinational Mining Corporations in Peru." *Journal of Peace Research* (1972): 189–207.

"Burke-Hartke Is Called a Wolf in Sheep's Clothing." *Chemical Marketing Reporter* 202 (October 9, 1972): 5+.

"Business Brief: Controlling the Multinationals." *The Economist* 258 (January 24, 1974): 68–69.

Byron, Christopher. "Congress vs. Milo Minderbinder." *World* 2 (January 16, 1973): 34.
On the bill in Congress to curtail the growth of U.S.-based multinationals, which some claim deprive Americans of jobs.

Calitri, J. C. "Challenge of Burke-Hartke." *Financial Executive* 40 (June 1972): 36–38.

Campos, Roberto de Oliveira. "Multinational Enterprise—Friend or Foe to Latin America." *Interplay* 4 (March 1971): 35–38.

Cateora, Philip R. "The Multinational Enterprise and Nationalism." *MSU Business Topics* 19 (Spring 1971): 49–56.

"Chemical and Pharmaceutical Men Now Mounting a Counter-Attack on Burke-Hartke Legislation." *Chemical Marketing Reporter* 202 (October 2, 1972): 3+.

Clark, Lindley H., Jr. "Global Crossroads: Multinational Firms, Under Fire All Over, Face a Changed Future." *The Wall Street Journal* 186 (December 3, 1975): 1+.

Clausen, A. W. "The International Corporation: An Executive's View." *The Annals of the American Academy of Political and Social Science* (September 1972).

Cummings, Joseph P. "Forging International Accounting Standards." *Tax Executive* 27 (July 1975): 352–359.

DeHahn, B. "Don't Hide—Be Specific with Company's Multinational Story." *Industrial Marketing* 59 (May 1974): 56.

Dehner, W. Joseph, Jr. "Multinational Enterprise and Racial Non-discrimination: United States Enforcement of an International Human Right." *Harvard International Law Journal* 15 (Winter 1974): 71–125.

Dillon, C. Douglas. "Cross-Cultural Communication Through the Arts." *Columbia Journal of World Business* 6 (September/October 1971): 31–38.

The multinational corporation continues the renaissance tradition of business patronage of the arts.

"Don't Worry, Nobody's Really Stealing Your Sovereignty." *The Economist* 244 (July 22, 1972): 80+.

Dufey, Gunter. "Myths About Multinational Corporations." *Michigan Business Review* 26 (May 1974): 10–17.

Eells, Richard. "Multinational Corporations Under Fire." *Management Review* 64 (Fall 1975): 43–45.

"Europeans Offer a Split Image of U.S. Multinationals." *Industry Week* 174 (July 17, 1972): 26–27.

Evans, Peter B. "National Autonomy and Economic Development: Critical Perspectives on Multinational Corporations in Poor Countries." *International Organization* 25 (Summer 1971): 675–692.

Ewing, David W. "The Corporation as Peacemonger." *Aramco World Magazine* 23 (March/April 1972): 22–25.

The political and social involvements of multinationals are discussed.

Ewing, David W. "MNC's on Trial." *Harvard Business Review* 50 (May/June 1972): 130–132+.

The literature on multinational companies reveals some of the risks, stakes and possible outcomes of future action.

Farrell, Richard J. and others. "Mounting Attacks on Multi-national Corporations." *Business Lawyer* 28 (March 1973): 241–288.

Fenley, J. J. "Multinationals Face Tougher Going." *Industry Week* 174 (August 28, 1972): 28–29+.

Gabriel, Peter P. "MNC's in the Third World: Is Conflict Unavoidable?" *Harvard Business Review* 50 (July/August 1972): 93–102.

The author analyzes the problem of growing resistance to direct investment by multinational companies in underdeveloped states.

Galloway, Jonathan. "The Military-Industrial Linkages of U.S. Based Multinational Corporations." *International Studies Quarterly* (December 1972): 491–510.

"The Global Corporation: Agent of Change." *Journal of International Law and Economics* 6 (January 1972): 211–267.

Green, R. T. and C. H. Smith. "Multinational Profitability as a Funciton for Political Instability." *Management International Review* 12 (1972): 23–29.

Grimes, J. A. "Multinationals: The Unknown Factors." *American Federationist* 80 (October 1973): 23–24.

Hall, C. R. "Mobilizing the Multinational." *Conference Board Record* 12 (July 1975): 47–48.

Heenan, David A. and Calvin Reynolds. "RPO's a Step Toward Global Human Resources Management." *California Management Review* 18 (Fall 1975): 5–9.
Regional personnel offices of multinational enterprises.

Heilbroner, Robert. "The Multinational Corporation and the Nation-State." *The New York Review of Books* (February 11, 1971).

Heilleiner, G. K. "The Role of Multinational Corporations in the Less Developed Countries' Trade in Technology." *World Development* 3 (April 1975): 161–189.
A discussion of the general character of the international market for technology. The role of the multinational in the transfer of both production and consumption technology and in developing more appropriate technologies for underdeveloped states is analyzed.

Hoadley, W. E. "Multinationalism in Fresh Perspective." *Bankers Monthly* 90 (July 1973): 4–6+.

Hobbing, Enno. "The World Corporation: A Catalytic Agent?" *Columbia Journal of World Business* 6 (July/August 1971): 45–51.
Presents the positive case for the world corporation as it relates to the impact it will have on man himself.

Howard, Cecil G. "The Extent of 'Nativization' of Management—A Worldwide Study." *Atlanta Economic Review* 21 (January 1971): 4–8.

"In Defense of the MNC's." *Management Review* 64 (June 1975): 56–59.

"Industry Takes on the World." *Industry Week* 168 (February 1, 1971): 36–40+.

Jackson, Sarah. "Oil MNCs: Are They in the National Interest?" *Columbia Journal of World Business* 9 (Fall 1974): 18–29.

Jaffe, E. D. "In Defense of MNC's Implications of Burke-Hartke." *MSU Business Topics* 21 (Summer 1973): 5–14.

Jager, Elizabeth R. "The Changing World of Multinationals." *American Federationist* 81 (September 1974): 17–24.

Janeway, Eliot. "Globaloney in a New Key." *Saturday Review* 2 (February 8, 1975): 21–24.
A review of the book by Richard Barnet and Ronald Muller— *Global Reach: The Power of the Multinational Corporations.*

Jantsch, Erich. "The 'World Corporation': The Total Commitment." *Columbia Journal of World Business* 6 (May/June 1971): 5–12.

Josephs, R. "Global Approach to Public Relations." *Columbia Journal of World Business* 8 (Fall 1973): 93–97.

Kaufman, K. A. "Multinationals: Mixed Curse or Blessing?" *Iron Age* 211 (March 8, 1973): 64–65.

Keohane, Robert O. and Van Doorn Ooms. "The Multinational Enterprise and World Political Economy." *International Organization* 26 (Winter 1972): 84+.

Kuin, Pieter. "The Magic of Multinational Management." *Harvard Business Review* 50 (November/December 1972): 89–97.
Multinational management lies not so much in perfection of methods or excellence of men as in developing respect for other nationalities and cultures.

Lawrence, F. G. "Multinationals Search for One World." *Industry Week* 176 (January 1, 1973): 1–16.

Lawrence, S. "Might and the Myths of the Multinationals." *Personnel Management* 6 (May 1974): 18–23.

Lea, David. "The International Company and Trade Union Interests." *Journal of Business Policy* 1 (Summer 1971): 30–39.
The article emphasizes how the internal decision-making structures of multinational companies can make it more difficult for trade unions to bargain effectively with them.

155

Lenhart, Harry, Jr. "Labor Fears Loss of Jobs in U.S. As Firms Expand Their Overseas Facilities." *National Journal* 3 (July 17, 1971): 1485–1493.

Longworth, Richard C. "Writing the Rule Book." *Saturday Review* (January 24, 1976): 24–30.
Laws should be formulated to control multinationals.

McNulty, Paul J. "The Predecessors of the Multinational Corporation." *Columbia Journal of World Business* (May-June 1972).

Madden, Carl H. "The Long-Range Future of Business." *The Futurist* 5 (February 1971): 5–8.
Multinational corporations may contribute to unification of the world and the end of nationalism. The role of corporations will be more important in performing social tasks and cause shifts in social values.

Maher, Jewel G. and Virginia Fiester. "The Multinationals: In the Land of the Giants, the Super-giants and the Super-Super Giants." *AAUW Journal of World Business* 9 (Spring 1974): 7–12.

Maisonrouge, J. G. "Mythology of Multinationalism." *Columbia Journal of World Business* 9 (Spring 1974): 7–12.

Mason, R. Hal. "Conflicts Between Host Countries and the Multinational Enterprise." *California Management Review* 17 (Fall 1974): 5–14.

Meyers, George. "US Trade Unions and the Multinationals." *New World Review* 39 (Spring 1971): 39–46.
A discussion of particular problems multinationals are creating for US workers and their impact on trade union policies.

Miller, J. Irwin. "Multinational Corporations: The UN Report." *Business Horizons* 17 (December 1974): 17–24.

Muller, Ronald E. "Globalization and the Failure of Economic Policy." *Challenge* (May-June 1975): 57–61.

Muller, Ronald. "Poverty Is the Product." *Foreign Policy* (*Winter* 1973/74).

"The Multinational Company." *Financial Executive* 41 (December 1973): 18–86.

"Multinational Drug Concerns Scored by European Unions." *Chemical Marketing Reporter* 204 (September 10, 1973): 5+.

"Multinational Furor Expected to Worsen." *Industry Week* 174 (September 4, 1972): 21–22+.

"Multinationals Are Not as Bad as All That." *The Economist* 248 (September 29, 1973): 91–92.

"Multinationals Deemed Threat to National Defense." *Chemical Marketing Reporter* 203 (March 12, 1973): 7+.

"Multinationals Find the Going Rougher." *Business Week* (July 14, 1975): 64–65+.

"Multinationals: Friend, Foe or Goat?" *Financial World* 138 (July 19, 1972): 3–4.

"Multinationals: Heroes? or Villains?" *Forbes* 111 (May 15, 1973): 264–269.

"Multinationals: How Patriotic?" *The Economist* 246 (January 6, 1973): 70.

"Multinationals in Asia: Conflict and Cooperation." *Multinational Business* (September 1973): 30–35.

"Multinationals Talk Their Way Out of Trouble." *Chemical Week* 112 (March 28, 1973): 18–19.

"Multinationals: The Public Gives Them Low Marks." *Business Week* (June 9, 1973): 42+.

"Multinationals Up for a Deep Think by Senate Panel." *Chemical Marketing Reporter* 203 (February 26, 1973): 5+.

"Multinationals Win Some Points." *Business Week* (March 3, 1973): 19–20.

Nader, Ralph and Mark J. Green. "Is the 'Worldcorp' Above the Law?" *War/Peace Report* 12 (October 1973): 3–7.

Ness, Walter L., Jr. "Brazil: Local Equity Participation in Multinational Enterprises." *Law and Policy in International Business* 6 (Fall 1974): 1017–1057.

"On the Way: Companies More Powerful than Nations." *US News and World Report* 71 (July 19, 1971): 38–41.

Pearson, J. "Domesticating the Multinationals." *Business Week* (May 26, 1973): 15.

Pearson, J. "Sovereignty vs. the Multinationals." *Business Week* (April 20, 1974): 22.

Robock, S. H. "The Case for Home Country Controls over Multinational Firms." *Columbia Journal of World Business* 9 (Summer 1974): 75–79.

Root, F. R. "Public Policy and the Multinational Corporation." *Business Horizons* 17 (April 1974): 67–78.

Root, F. R. "Public Policy Expectations of Multinational Managers." *MSU Business Topics* 21 (Autumn 1973): 5–12.

Rubin, Seymour J. "Multinational Enterprise and National Sovereignty: A Skeptic's Analysis." *Law and Policy in International Business* 3 (1971): 1–41.

Safarian, A. E. and J. Bell. "Issues Raised by National Control of the Multinational Corporation." *Columbia Journal of World Business* 8 (Winter 1973): 7–18.

Sarnoff, R. W. "Maligned Multinational: Key to a Better Third World." *Commercial and Financial Chronicle* 220 (October 27, 1975): 12.

Searle, Bruce A. "Is My Transfer a Promotion, Demotion or Lateral Move?" *Worldwide Projects and Industry Planning* 5 (July/August 1971): 35+.
  The article discusses the need for a common salary grading system in the multinational firm and how to achieve it.

Sharman, Ben. "A Trade Unionist View of Multinational Corporations." *Worldview* 18 (November 1975): 31–35.

"Shedding Some Light on Myths About Multinationals." *Multinational Business* (July 1975): 42–45.

Shevis, James M. "The Web of Corporate Corruption." *American Federationist* 82 (October 1975): 5–10.
  The alleged massive under-the-table payoffs to foreign officials and political parties by United States-based multinational corporations are discussed.

Sirota, David and J. Michael Greenwood. "Understanding Your Overseas Work Force." *Harvard Business Review* 49 (January/February

1971): 53–60.
Successful multinational management hinges on an objective, informed assessment of what foreign employees really want from their jobs.

Stevens, Robert Warren. "Scanning the Multinational Firm: Profiles, Problems, and Prospects." *Business Horizons* 14 (June 1971): 47–54.

Stinson, R. J. "Global Giants Under Heavy Fire." *Financial World* 139 (April 18, 1973): 4–5+.

Stobaugh, Robert B. "The Hidden Pluses of Multinationals." *Wall Street Journal* 181 (June 6, 1976): 20.

Stobaugh, Robert B. "The Multinational Corporation: Measuring the Consequences." *Columbia Journal of World Business* 6 (January 1971): 59–64.

Trezise, Philip H. "Some Policy Implications of the Multinational Corporations," *Department of State Bulletin* 64 (May 24, 1971): 669–672.

Turner, Louis. "Multinational Companies and the Third World." *World Today* 30 (September 1974): 394–402.

Turner, Louis. "The Multinational Company: Some Social and Political Implications." *Journal of Business Policy* 2 (Autumn 1971): 49–55.

Tyler, Gus. "Multinationals: A Global Menace." *American Federationist* 79 (July 1972): 1–7.

"US Multinationalism: An Illusory Threat." *Business Week* (October 19, 1974): 19+.

Vernon, Raymond. "The Multinational Enterprise: Power Versus Sovereignty." *Foreign Affairs* 49 (July 1971): 736–751.

Villanueva, R. T. "Case For and Against the Multinationals." *Conference Board Record* 10 (November 1973): 61–63.

Warner, Rawleigh. "What Doth It Profit a Man." *Saturday Review* (January 24, 1976): 20–57.
Multinationals are in business to profit themselves and the world, argues a chief executive officer of Mobil Oil Corporation.

Weinshall, T. D. "Multinational Corporations—Their Development and Universal Role." *Management International Review* 15 (1975): 17–28.

Welles, John G. "Multinationals Need New Environmental Strategies." *Columbia Journal of World Business* 8 (Summer 1973): 11–18.
   Multinationals and industrialized nations stand to gain by greater harmonization of environmental actions among nations. The author suggests that they should capitalize on their common interests by working together rather than independently.

Wells, Louis T., Jr. "The Multinational Business Enterprise: What Kind of International Organization?" *International Organization* 25 (Summer 1971): 447–464.

Wells, Louis T., Jr. "Social Cost/Benefit Analysis for MNCs." *Harvard Business Review* 53 (March 1975): 40–42+.

"What Is the Case Against Multinationals?" *Multinational Business* (April 1975): 1–12.

"Who Controls MNCs?" *Harvard Business Review* 53 (November 1975): 97–108.
   An interview with Citicorp's W. I. Spencer.

Woodroofe, E. "The Social Role of Multinational Enterprises." *Conference Board Record* 10 (November 1973): 57-60.

Wright, Richard W. "Is the Multinational Firm in Danger?" *Business Horizons* 14 (April 1971): 31-34.

Wrioton, Walter B. "World Corporations: Saints or Sinners?" *Business and Society Review/Innovation* (Winter 1973/1974): 82–85.

Yergin, Daniel. "The One-Man Flying Multinational." *The Atlantic Monthly* 235 (June 1975): 31–43.
   First article in two part series—story of Armand Hammer's rise in power/economic & political.

Yergin, Daniel. "The One-Man Flying Multinational." *The Atlantic Monthly* 236 (July 1975): 55–68.
   Second of a two part series, describing the wheeling and dealing of Armand Hammer.

Zenoff, David B. "The Future of the Multinational Corporation." *Euromoney* (September 1975): 146+.

Safety and Health

Books

Bureau of National Affairs, Washington, D.C. *OSHA and the Unions; Bargaining on Job Safety and Health*. Washington, 1973.

Cralley, Lester V., ed. *Industrial Environmental Health: The Worker and the Community*. New York: Academic Press, 1972.

Gausch, John P. *Balanced Involvement: Safety, Production, Motivation*. Park Ridge, Illinois: American Society of Safety Engineers, 1973.

Matschulat, James O. and John P. Gausch. *Organizing for OSHAct: A Management Challenge*. New York: ANACOM, 1973.

Occupational Safety and Health. A transcript of a MAPI Seminar. Washington, D.C.: Machinery & Allied Products Institute (1200 Eighteenth Street, N.W.), 1973.
A comprehensive picture of what is happening in industry regarding occupational safety and health.

Page, Joseph A. and Mary Win O'Brien. *Bitter Wages: Ralph Nader's Study Group Report on Disease and Injury on the Job*. New York: Grossman, 1973.

Widner, Joanne T., ed. *Selected Readings in Safety*. Macon, Ga.: Academy Press, 1973.
A collection of articles by leaders in the safety and loss control profession.

Williford, Frederick L. *The OSHA Dilemma: An Analysis of the Citation and Penalty System as an Incentive to Comply with the Occupational Safety and Health Act*. Washington: Heritage Foundation, 1974.

Articles

"Animosity over Asbestos (Pittsburgh-Corning)." *Chemical Week* 110 (February 23, 1972): 17.

Ashford, N. A. "Worker Health and Safety: An Area of Conflicts." *Monthly Labor Review* 98 (September 1975): 3-11.

Austin, Danforth W. "Industrial Headache: Factory Workers Grow

Increasingly Rebellious over Noise Pollution." *Wall Street Journal* 179 (June 14, 1972): 1+.

  Ten million may hear poorly from excess of sound; plus evidence of more ills.

Beck, Steve. "Industrial Poison." *International Socialist Review* 35 (December 1974): 26–32.

  What has and has not been done to safeguard employees in their work.

Bishop, T. "Hazards, Health and Hygiene." *Personnel Management* 3 (September 1971): 37+.

Bresnahan, Margaret. "What Went Wrong with Tom Fox's Shiney New Ford Torino." *Saturday Review* 55 (June 17, 1972): 5–12.

  On the Ford Motor Company's negligence in manufacturing faulty cars, then not promptly fixing them or compensating for the inconvenience of buyers.

Conn, Harry. "Quieting Ear Pollution." *American Federationist* 82 (October 1975): 21–24.

  Discusses tolerable level of industrial noise.

Cordtz, Dan. "Safety on the Job Becomes a Major Job for Management." *Fortune* 86 (November 1972): 112–117+.

Culhane, Charles. "Occupational Safety Agency Weighs Emergency Standards for Chemical Compounds." *National Journal* 5 (April 21, 1973): 567-570.

  Products suspected of causing cancer among workers.

Donnelly, J. J. "OSHA Men Almost Sure to Drop In: Preparation for Visit Pays Off." *National Underwriter Property and Casualty Insurance Edition* 77 (March 30, 1973): 1+.

Fair, Richard S. "Aspirin: Good News, Bad News." *Saturday Review of Science* 55 (December 1972): 60–63.

  Advertisements do not tell us the harmful effects of aspirin.

"Fight Against Noise on the Job—A Health Hazard You Can't See; Latest Uproar over Environment." *US News and World Report* 78 (May 26, 1975): 77–78.

  How much money should business be required to spend to quiet their factories, shops offices?

162

"Final Rules Set for Exposure to Carcinogens." *Chemical and Engineering News* 52 (February 11, 1974): 12–13.

Gardner, A. R. "Hearing Protection: New Law, and Problems." *Machinery* 78 (May 1972): 60–61.

Gillette, Robert. "Plutonium: Questions of Health in a New Industry." *Science* 185 (September 20, 1974): 1027–1032.

Grimes, Richard M. and Michael Decker. "Health Services and the Corporation." *University of Michigan Business Review* 27 (July 1975): 16–19.

Hall, L. "Health Hazard That Won't Come Clean in the Wash." *"Engineer* 235 (August 10, 1972): 47–48.

"Hi, Joe! How're You Feeling?" *Industry Week* 174 (August 7, 1972): 28–32.

"Hi, Joe! How's the Ol' Ticker?" *Industry Week* 174 (August 14, 1972): 48–50+.

"How the Safety Act Affects Banks." *Banking* 64 (May 1972): 60–64+.

Hyatt, James C. "Jobs and Health: U.S. Mulls Rules for Handling of Chemicals that Can Lead to Cancer in Plant Workers." *Wall Street Journal* 181 (April 11, 1973): 42.

Judd, Stanley H. "Noise Abatement in Process Plants." *Chemical Engineering* 78 (January 11, 1971): 139-145.

Kelsey, P. "Asbestos Exposure: How Serious a Health Problem Is It?" *Air Conditioning, Heating and Refrigeration News* 129 (May 14, 1973): 1+.

Key, Marcus M. "New Horizons in Industrial Health." *Health Services Reports* 88 (March 1973): 195–200.

Kobler, Jay. "Omnibus Bill: Good or Bad for Management?" *Environmental Control and Safety Management* 141 (April 1971): 16–18+.

Kobler, Jay. "Organized Labor Acts on the Omnibus Bill." *Environmental Control and Safety Management* 141 (May 1971): 20–23.

Lyons, J. M. "Safety: The Company, The Committee and the Committed." *Personnel Journal* 51 (February 1972): 95–98+.

McCormick, W. E. "Environmental Health Control for the Rubber Industry." *Rubber Chemistry and Technology* 44 (April 1971): 512–533.

Mayfield, H. "Safety a Matter of Attitudes." *Supervisory Management* 16 (February 1971): 15–16.

Moran, Robert D. "How to Obtain Job Safety Justice." *Labor Law Journal* 24 (July 1973): 387–405.

Moran, Robert D. "Our Job Safety Law School Should Say What It Means." *Nation's Business* 62 (April 1974): 23–26.

"More Firms Willing to Sell Industrial Safety Expertise." *Industry Week* 174 (July 3, 1972): 16+.

Mossberg, Walter. "Jobs and Safety: More Unions Devote Efforts to Eliminating Hazards in Work Place." *Wall Street Journal* 184 (August 19, 1974): 7+.
Accident prevention, health become contract issues.

Nilsen, Joan M. "OSHA: Acronym for Trouble." *Chemical Engineering* 79 (March 20, 1972): 58–60.

"OCAW, Nader's Group Sue US on Carcinogens." *Chemical Marketing Reporter* 203 (April 30, 1973): 5+.

"Occupational Health Looming as Major Problem for Rubber Industry." *Rubber World* 172 (May 1975): 66–68+.

Oravec, John R. "The Continuing Fight for Job Safety." *American Federationist* 81 (June 1974): 1–6.

"OSHA Says Metalworking Dust Is Not to Be Sneezed At." *Iron Age* 215 (February 17, 1975): 45–46.

Peterson, Russell W. "Role of Toxic Substances on Our Environmental Health." *Journal of Environmental Science* 17 (May 1974): 27–30.

"Plastics, the Law, and You: Plastics and Occupational Health and Safety." *Plastics Engineering* 30 (March 1974): 25–29.

"Purchasing—OSHA's Man in the Middle." *Purchasing* 74 (February 6, 1973): 37–49.

Ratliff, T. A., Jr. "Quality Control in Occupational Safety and Health." *Professional Safety* 20 (January 1975): 47–51.

Riech, Bill. "Noise and the Occupational Safety and Health Act." *Environmental Control and Safety Management* 142 (July 1971): 12–17.

"Safety and Health." *Panorama* (1st Quarter, 1971).
The entire issue is devoted to occupational safety and health problems.

"Safety and Industrial Hygiene as Aids to Efficient Chemical Plant Practice." *Chemical and Industry* (April 20, 1974): 328–333.

"Should Firms Pay Out for Unsafe Products" *Industry Week* 174 (September 4, 1972): 18–19.

Steiger, William A. "Omnibus Bill: A Bitter Past; A Better Future?" *Environmental Control and Safety Management* 141 (June 1971): 11–15+.

Suchocki, Carl J. "All About OSHA—or Don't Press Your Luck." *Iron Age* 208 (December 16, 1971): 68–69.

Summar, M. T. Implementation of a Hearing Preservation Program." *American Paper Industry* 55 (November 1973): 16–18+.

Swift, R. L. "New Law Spurs Importance of Noise Pollution Control." *Petro/Chemical Engineer* 43 (March 1971): 22–23.

Vandivier, Kermit. "The Aircraft Brake Scandal." *Harper's Magazine* 244 (April 1972): 45–52.
An account of attempted fraud by the B. F. Goodrich Company in trying to sell a faulty brake.

"Who Cares? Riegel Textile, for One." *Textile World* 122 (February 1972): 44–5.

William, Douglas N. "Working May Be Hazardous to Your Health." *Iron Age* 209 (January 20, 1972): 22–23.

Williams, Harrison A., Jr. "Legislation and Responsibility: The Occupational Safety and Health Act." *Journal of Current Social Issues* 12 (Spring 1975): 13–17.

Williford, Frederick L. "Voluntarism: OSHA's Missing Link." *Association Management* 27 (March 1975): 53–57.
Need for voluntary compliance with the provisions of the Occupational Safety & Health Act of 1970.

Wilson, R. A. "Safety Act: Unsafe at Any Reading." *Iron Age* 207 (June 10, 1971): 67–68.

Wolnez, George J. "Safety Policy: A Negative Approach for Positive Results." *Management Review* 60 (January 1971): 17–21.

Social Audit

Books

Bauer, Raymond A. and Dan H. Fenn, Jr. *The Corporate Social Audit*. New York: Russell Sage Foundation, 1972.
A comprehensive discussion of the issues, problems, and promises of social accounting.

Corson, John C. and George Steiner. *Measuring Business Social Performance: The Corporate Social Audit*. Committee for Economic Development, 1974.

Dieres, Meinolf and Raymond A. Bauer, eds. *Corporate Social Accounting*. New York: Praeger, 1973.

Humble, John. *Social Responsibility Audit: A Management Tool for Survival*. New York: American Management Associations, 1973.

Linowes, David F. *The Corporate Conscience*. New York: Hawthorn Books, Incorporated, 1974.

Believing that profits alone do not measure effective performance, the author presents a proposal for a Socio-Economic Operating Statement that would detail corporate expenditures aimed at advancing the welfare of employees and the public, product safety and environmental balance.

Articles

Abt, Clark C. "Managing the Socially Responsible Corporation: New Accounting Tools." *Garrett Lecture, Columbia University Graduate School of Business,* January, 1973.

Abt, Clark K. "Managing to Save Money While Doing Good." *Innovation* 27 (January, 1972): 38–47.

"Accounting for Corporate Social Performance." *Management Accounting* 55 (February 1974): 39–41.

Andrews, Frederick. "Changing Times: Puzzled Businessmen Ponder New Methods of Measuring Success." *The Wall Street Journal* 178 (December 9, 1971): 1+.
Profit statements alone are criticized as not showing companies' social impact.

Anthony, R. N. "Accounting for the Cost of Equity." *Harvard Business Review* 51 (November 1973): 88–102.

Barnett, A. H. and J. C. Caldwell. "Accounting for Corporate Social Performance: A Survey." *Management Accounting* 56 (November 1974): 23–26.

Bauer, Raymond A. "Corporate Social Audit: Getting on the Learning Curve." *California Management Review* 16 (Fall 1973): 5–10.

Bauer, Raymond A. "Corporate Social Audit: Where Does It Stand Today?" *Personnel* 50 (July 1973): 8–18.

Bauer, Raymond A. and Dan H. Fenn, Jr. "What Is a Corporate Social Audit?" *Harvard Business Review* 51 (January 1973): 37–48.

Bendock, C. M. "Measuring Social Costs." *Management Accounting* 56 (January 1975): 13–15.

Butcher, B. L. "Program Management Approach to the Corporate Social Audit." [Bank of America, San Francisco]. *California Management Review* 16 (Fall 1973): 11–16.

Cerisano, M. P. "SMS: Social Measurement Systems for the Future— A Practitioner's Preview." *The CPA Journal* 44 (May 1974): 25–30.

Clausen, A. W. "Toward an Arithmetic of Quality." *Conference Board Record* 8 (May 1971): 9–13.

"Committee on Accounting for Corporate Social Performance." *Management Accounting* 56 (September 1974): 59–60.

Cooper, S. Kerry and Mitchell H. Raiborn. "Accounting for Corporate Social Responsibility." *MSU Business Topics* 22 (Spring 1974): 19–26.

Dilley, S. C. "Case of the Nebulous Numbers (Social Audit)." *Harvard Business Review* 52 (November 1974): 42–44+.

Dilley, S. C. "Practical Approaches to Social Accounting." *The CPA Journal* 45 (February 1975): 17–21.

Dilley, S. C. and J. J. Weygandt. "Measuring Social Responsibility: An Empirical Test." *Journal of Accountancy* 136 (September 1973): 62–70.

Eiteman, Dean S. "Critical Problems in Accounting for Goodwill." *Journal of Accountancy* 131 (March 1971): 46–50.

Elias, N. and M. Epstein. "Dimensions of Corporate Social Reporting." *Management Accounting* 56 (March 1975): 36–40.

Elliott, R. K. and S. I. Rosenthal. "Social Accounting—An Annotated Bibliography." *Journal of Accountancy* 136 (July 1973): 75–79.

"First Attempts at a Corporate Social Audit." *Business Week* (September 23, 1972): 88–89+.

Gilbert, G. T. "Accounting for Goodwill—Anything Goes." *Canadian Chartered Accountant* 98 (April 1971): 250–255.

Goldston, Eli. "Toward Social Accounting." *Annual Report* (Eastern Gas and Fuel Associates), 1972.

Gray, D. H. "Methodology: One Approach to the Corporate Social Audit." *California Management Review* 15 (Summer 1973): 106–109.

Humble, John. "Getting Ready for the Social Responsibility Audit." *The Director* 25 (February 1973): 176–180.

"Keeping Book on Social Action." *Business Week* (October 14, 1972): 94+.

Keller, I. W. "Planning Corporate Social Performance." *Management Accounting* 56 (June 1975): 19–24.

Lilley, Robert D. "Society and the Balance Sheet." *Bell Telephone Magazine* 50 (September/October 1971): 6–8+.

Linowes, David F. "Let's Get On with the Social Audit: A Specific Proposal." *Business and Society Review* 4 (Winter 1972): 39–42.

Lowes, B. and J. R. Sparkes. "Fitting Accounting to Social Goals." *Business Horizons* 17 (June 1974): 53–57.

"Measuring Costs of Social Action." *Management Accounting* 56 (September 1975): 60.

Nolan, J. "San Francisco CPAs Work in the Public Interest." *Journal of Accounting* 136 (August 1973): 24+.

Novick, David. "Cost-benefit Analysis and Social Responsibility." *Business Horizons* 16 (October 1973): 63-72.

Pick, J. "Is Responsibility Accounting Irresponsible?" *The New York Certified Public Accountant* 41 (July 1971): 487–494.

"Report of the Committee on the Measurement of Social Costs, American Accounting Association." *Accounting Review* 49 supplement (1974): 98–113.

Rockefeller, Rodman C. "Turn Public Problems to Private Accounts." *Harvard Business Review* 49 (January/February 1971): 131–138.

Schrivener, R. C. "Cautions on Social Accounting and Responsibility." *The CPA Journal* 44 (January 1974): 17–19.

Schrivener, R. C. "Social Accounting—Sharing the Responsibility." *Financial Executive* 42 (January 1974): 24–27.

Sethi, S. Prakash. "Getting a Handle on the Social Audit." *Business and Society Review/Innovation* (Winter 1972/1973): 31–38.

Shulman, J. S. and J. Gale. "Laying the Groundwork for Social Accounting." *Financial Executive* 40 (March 1972): 38–42.

"Social Audit Begins to Move." *Industry Week* 178 (August 20, 1973): 42+.

"Social Responsibility Reporting." *The CPA Journal* 44 (December 1974): 71–72.

Stahl, Sheldon W. "Social Costs: The Due Bill for Progress." *Federal Reserve Kansas City* (April 1972): 13–19.

Steiner, George A. "Should Business Adopt the Social Audit?" *Conference Board Record* 9 (May 1972): 7–10.

Taft, R. W. and C. S. Thompson. "New Requirements in Corporate Reporting." *Public Relations Journal* 27 (April 1971): 10–14.

Tearney, Michael G. "Accounting for Goodwill: A Realistic Approach." *Journal of Accountancy* 136 (July 1973): 41–45.

Toan, Arthur B., Jr. "Measuring the Social Performance of Business." *Price Waterhouse Review* 18 (1973): 4–9.

"Toan Says Committee Tries to Integrate Social, Financial Reports." *Management Advisor* 10 (March 1973): 14.

Truex, G. Robert. "Measuring the Social Performance of Banks." *Trusts and Estates* 112 (August 1973): 566–568.

vonBerg, W. G. "Accounting for Responsibility." *Journal of Accountancy* 134 (November 1972): 71–74.

Walker, C. W. "Profit Ability and Responsibility Accounting." *Management Accounting* 53 (December 1971): 23–30.

Walton, C. "Public Auditors Must Weigh Society's Needs." *Management Advisor* 9 (March 1972): 13.

Weaver, K. Mark and Denise Vlcek. "Views on the Corporate Social Audit." *Carroll Business Bulletin* 14 (Fall 1974): 10–17.

Weiner, David P. "Accountants for the Public Interest: A Brief History." *The CPA Journal* (March 1975): 18+.

Woefel, C. J. "Exploring Opportunities in Social Accounting." *The CPA Journal* 43 (November 1973): 1006–1007.

United States Business Abroad

Books

Barnet, Richard J. *Intervention and Revolution.* New York: Mentor, 1972.

Basche, James R. Jr. *Unusual Foreign Payments: A Survey of the Policies and Practices of U.S. Companies. The Conference Board Report,* 682, New York, New York, 1976.

Behrman, Jack N. *U.S. International Business and Government.* New York: McGraw-Hill, 1971.

Behrman, Jack N. and others. *International Business-Government Communications: U.S. Structures, Actors, and Issues.* Lexington: D. C. Heath and Company, 1975.
Ways United States businesses abroad interact with United States

embassies and with most governments, thereby potentially impinging on the formation of United States foreign policies.

Berg, Alan. *The Nutrition Factor: Its Role in National Development.* Washington, D.C.: The Brookings Institution, 1973.

Bhagwati, Jagdish, ed. *Economics and World Order.* Columbia, Missouri: South Asia Books, 1973.

Blair, John M. *Economic Concentration: Structure, Behavior and Public Policy.* New York: Harcourt Brace Jovanovich, 1972.

Boddewyn, Jean and others. *World Business Systems and Environments* New York: Intext Educational Publishers, 1972.

The Effects of U.S. Corporate Foreign Investment: 1960-1970. New York: Business Internation Special Research Study, 1972.

Gunneman, Jon P., ed. *The Nation-State and Transnational Corporations in Conflict: With Special Reference to Latin America.* New York: Praeger, 1975.

Günter, Hans, ed. *Transnational Industrial Relations.* London: Macmillan, 1973.
    This covers a symposium of the International Institute of Labor Studies.

Kapor, Ashok and Jean J. Boddewyn. *International Business-Government Relations: U.S. Corporate Experience in Asia and Western Europe.* New York: American Management Associations, 1973.

Keohane, Robert O. and Joseph S. Nye Jr., eds. *Transnational Relations and World Politics.* Cambridge, Massachusetts: Harvard Universtiy Press, 1972.
    See the article, "Labor and Transnational Relations" by Robert W. Cox for a good overview of bibliographic sources.

Kolko, Gabriel. *The Limits of Power: The World and U.S. Foreign Policy.* New York: Harper and Row, 1972.

Penrose, Edith. *Growth of Firms, Middle East Oil and Other Essays.* Portland, Oregon: International Scholarly Book Service, 1971.

South Africa, A National Profile. Ernst nad Ernst International Business Series, May 1971.

171

Wells, Louis T. Jr., ed. *The Product Life Cycle and International Trade.* Boston, Massachusetts: Harvard Graduate School of Business Administration, Harvard University, 1972.

Wilber, Charles K., ed. *The Political Economy of Development and Underdevelopment.* New York: Random House, 1973.

Wilson, Joan. *American Business and Foreign Policy: 1920-1933.* Lexington, Kentucky: University Press of Kentucky, 1971.

Articles

Behrman, Jack N. "Foreign vs. Local Ownership." *Worldview* 17 (September 1974): 39–46.
Emphasis is on the role of business abroad and the United States government.

Bender, Marylin. "Ethics Experts Wax Inconclusive on Bribery Abroad." *The New York Times* (August 3, 1975), Section 3, p. 1.

Blashill, John. "The Proper Role of U.S. Corporations in South Africa." *Fortune* (July 1972).

Blundell, William and Stephen Sansweet. "On the Give: For U.S. Firms Abroad." *Wall Street Journal* 185 (May 9, 1975): 1+.

"Bribery, Corruption, or Necessary Fees and Charges?" *Multinational Business* (September 1975): 1–17.
Ethical aspects of U.S. multinationals' use of political contributions and payment of agents or consultants fees as means of promoting foreign business or obtaining special favors.

Carley, William M. "When in Rome—." *Wall Street Journal* 185 (May 19, 1975): 1+.
Oil Company gifts to political parties in Rome.

"Confrontations Between Industry, Critics Grow." *Industry Week* 168 (February 15, 1971): 13–14.
A discussion of Polaroid's business practices in South Africa.

"Corporate Rush to Confess All." *Business Week* (February 23, 1976): 22–24.

Daniels, John D. "The Non-American Manager, Especially as Third Country National in U.S. Multinationals." *Journal of International*

172

Business Studies 5 (Fall 1974): 25–40.
Unequal treatment for foreign managers has been common.

Dickinson, Richard D. N. "World Economic Development and the Question of Justice." *World Justice* 12 (June 1971): 435–449.

Donnelly, J. H., Jr. "Attitudes Toward Culture and Approach to International Advertising." *Journal of Marketing* 34 (July 1970): 60–3.

Ewing, David W. "The Corporation as Peacemonger." *Aramco World Magazine* 23 (March/April 1972): 22–25.

Fantl, I. L. "Case Against International Uniformity." *Management Accounting* 52 (May 1971): 13-16.

Grollman, W. K. "Independence of Auditors and Applicability of International Engagements." *The CPA Journal* 43 (April 1973): 286–291.

Gwirtzman, Milton S. "Is Bribery Defensible?" *The New York Times Magazine* (October 5, 1975): 19, 100–110.
The author, an international lawyer, sees bribery in the international market place as a difficult and complex issue from the perspective of ethics, law, business and statecraft. Aside from being informative, normative judgements are offered.

Henshaw, John H. "Problems of Doing Business Abroad: A Management Perspective." *Pittsburgh Business Review* 41 (March/April 1971): 1–6.

Howell, Leon. "Southeast Asia: The Solid American Presence." *Christianity and Crisis* 35 (June 23, 1975): 156–157.

Margulies, Leah. "Baby Formula Abroad: Exporting Infant Malnutrition." *Christianity and Crisis* 35 (November 10, 1975): 264–267.

Meeker, Guy. "Made-out Joint Venture: Can It Work for Latin America?" *Inter American Economic Affairs* (Spring 1971): 25–42.

"Polaroid to Continue South African Program to Aid Black Workers." *Wall Street Journal* (December 31, 1971).

Vaitsos, Constantine. "Patents Revisited: Their Function in Developing Countries." *Journal of Development Studies.* (October 1972).

Wideman, Bernard. "Banana Boom: Fruits for Only a Few." *Far Eastern Economic Review* (January 21, 1974): 52–52.

"World Trade: A U.S. Ambassador's New Business Role." *Business Week* (December 16, 1972): 38.

173

Theoretical and Applied Ethics

Theoretical and Applied Ethics

Books

Barnsley, John H. *Social Reality of Ethics: The Comparative Analysis of Moral Codes*. London: Routledge, 1972.
  A helpful, but not conclusive attempt at a definition of morality.

Barry, Brian. *The Liberal Theory of Justice*. New York: Oxford University Press, 1974.

Beauchamp, Tom L. *Ethics and Public Policy*. Englewood Cliffs, New Jersey: Prentice Hall, 1975.

Bedau, Hugo A., ed. *Justice and Equality*. Englewood Cliffs, New Jersey: Prentice Hall, 1971.

Bowie, Norman E. *Towards a New Theory of Distributive Justice*. Amherst, Massachusetts: University of Massachusetts Press, 1971.

Callahan, Daniel. *The Tyranny of Survival*. New York: Macmillan, 1973.
  An examination of the social and ethical implications of scientific-technological advance today.

Colson, Elizabeth. *Tradition and Contract: The Problem of Order*. Chicago, Illinois: Aldine Publishing, 1974.

Feinberg, Joel. *Doing and Deserving: Essays in the Theory of Responsibility*. Princeton, New Jersey: Princeton University Press, 1974.

Ferkiss, Victor C. *The Future of Technological Civilization*. New York: George Braziller, 1974.

Finkelstein, Louis, ed. *Social Responsibility in an Age of Revolution*. New York: Jewish Theological Seminary, 1971.
  An interesting anthology with a chapter on "Business Ethics."

Frankena, William K. *Ethics*. 2nd edition. Englewood Cliffs, New Jersey: Prentice Hall, 1973.
    A succinct treatment of ethical theories.

Frankena, William K. and John T. Granrose, eds. *Introductory Readings in Ethics*. Englewood Cliffs, New Jersey: Prentice Hall, 1974.

French, Peter A. *Individual and Collective Responsibility*. Cambridge, Massachusetts: Shenkman, 1972.

Grisez, Germain and Russell Shaw. *Beyond the New Morality*. South Bend: University of Notre Dame Press, 1974.
    The authors argue against situtaion ethics and in favor of a deontological approach.

Gustafson, James M. *Theology and Christian Ethics*. Philadelphia, Pennsylvania: United Church Press, 1974.

Hardin, Garrett. *Exploring New Ethics for Survival: The Voyage of the Spaceship Beagle*. Baltimore, Maryland: Penquin Books, 1972.
    This renowned biologist sets forth a version of "life boat ethics" as applicable to the world political, economic and ecologic situation. If not all can live, who should live? "The responsible ones," is Hardin's answer.

Hare, R. M. *Essays in Moral Concepts*. New York: Macmillan, 1972.

Jersild, Paul T. and Dale A. Johnson, eds. *Moral Issues and Christian Response*. New York: Holt, Rinehart and Winston, 1971 (revised 1976).

Johnson, James and David Smith. *Love and Society: Essays in the Ethics of Paul Ramsey*. Missoula, Montana: Scholars Press, 1974.
    The essays evaluate and elucidate the thought of a leading Christian ethicist. The volume opens up many avenues of ethical theory and application.

Jonas, Hans. Philosophical Essays: *From Ancient Creed to Technological Man*. Englewood Cliffs, New Jersey: Prentice Hall, 1974.
    This distinguished philosopher and social theorist has put together eighteen essays that touch in a variety of ways issues of ethics, value, religion and social responsibility.

Kaufman, Walter. *Without Guilt and Justice*. New York: Dell, 1975.

Ladd, John. *Ethical Relativism*. Belmont, California: Wadsworth, 1973.

Leiser, Burton M. *Liberty, Justice, and Morals: Contemporary Value Conflicts.* New York: Macmillan, 1973.

An anthology of essays focusing on specific cases and theoretical ethical reasoning. Part three is especially relevant to business ethics.

Lineberry, William P. *Justice in America: Law, Order, and the Courts.* New York: H. W. Wilson, 1972.

Menger, Karl. *Morality, Decision and Social Organization.* Boston: Reidel, 1974.

A theoretical construction toward the logic of ethics.

Nozick, Robert. *Anarchy, State and Utopia.* New York: Basic Books, 1974.

The author recommends an integration of ethics, legal philosophy and economic theory and a new theory of distributive justice. He argues for a very limited involvement of government.

Outka, Gene and John P. Reeder Jr. *Religion and Morality.* New York: Doubleday, 1973.

An informative collection of essays including both religious and philosophical discussions. The opening essay on "Definitions of Religion and Morality" by David Little and Summer B. Twiss is an articulate contribution.

Passmore, John. *Man's Responsibility for Nature.* New York: Charles Scribner, 1974.

Phelps, Edmund S., ed. *Altruism, Morality, and Economic Theory.* New York: Russell Sage Foundation, 1975.

A very helpful collection of articles by such authors as Kenneth Arrow, William Baumol, Thomas Nagle, Pete Hammond, *et. al.*

Pitkin, Hanna Fenichel. *Wittgenstein and Justice.* Los Angeles, California: University of California Press, 1972.

Pospisil, Leopold. *Anthropology of Law.* New York: Harper and Row, 1971.

And informative volume on how the legal profession makes decisions and justifies decisions.

Quinton, Anthony M. *Utilitarian Ethics.* New York: St. Martins Press, 1973.

Rawls, John. *A Theory of Justice.* Cambridge, Massachusetts: Harvard University Press, 1971.

179

A fresh constructive treatment of the concept of justice as fairness. This is a comprehensive philosophical treatment with special relevance to the economic order and business life.

Singer, Marcus G. *Generalization in Ethics: An Essay in the Logic of Ethics, with the Rudiments of a System of Moral Philosophy.* New York: Atheneum, 1971.

Skinner, B. F. *Beyond Freedom and Dignity.* New York: Knopf, 1972.

Smart, J. J. C. and Bernard Williams. *Utilitarianism: For and Against.* New York: Cambridge University Press, 1973.

Struhl, Karshen J. and Paula Rothenberg Struhl, eds. *Ethics in Perspective.* New York: Random House, 1975.
This is a comprehensive reader on theoretical ethics and contemporary moral problems including one section on "Business Ethics and Social Responsibility."

Wasserstrom, Richard. *Today's Moral Problems.* New York: Macmillan Co., 1975.
A collection of writings by distinguished philosophers on concrete moral issues. Most of the articles represent normative ethical reflection

Williams, Bernard. *Morality: An Introduction to Ethics.* New York: Harper and Row, 1972.

Articles

Ake, Christopher. "Justice as Equality." *Philosophy and Public Affairs* 5 (Fall 1975): 69–89.
A substantive article on the substance of justice as a norm applicable to all societies.

Becker, Lawrence C. "The Neglect of Virtue." *Ethics* 85 (January 1975): 110–122.
A plea for virtue and greater attention to "the good person" agent theory of ethics.

Bok, Sissela and Paul Ramsey. "The Leading Edge of the Wedge." *Hastings Center Report* 1 (December 1971): 9–12.

Brooks, Harvey. "Technology and Values: New Ethical Issues Raised by Technological Progress." *Zygon* 8 (March 1973): 17–35.

Clark, Henry. "Intuitionism and Situationism." *Soundings* (Winter 1975): 499–505.
This is a romping criticism of intuitionism and a modest defensive of situation ethics (understood as summary rule-agapism).

Clark, Henry. "Justice as Fairness and Christian Ethics." *Soundings* (Fall 1973): 359–369.
The author distinguishes between social ethics and the ethics of interpersonal relationships. The former can be something of a science; the latter is more of an art.

Edel, Abraham. "Scientists, Partisans and Social Conscience." *Transaction* 9 (January 1972): 33–39.

Frankl, Charles. "The Nature and Sources of Irrationalism." *Science* 180 (June 1, 1973): 927–931.

Goodin, Robert E. "How to Determine Who Should Get What." *Ethics* 85 (July 1975): 310–321.
An essay on making ethical judgment.

Green, Harold P. "Human Values in a Technological Society." *Dimensions in American Judaism* 5 (Winter 1971): 19–23.

Herberg, Will. "The 'What' and 'How' in Ethics." *Modern Age* 15 (Fall 1971): 350–357.
The thesis of this eminent social philosopher is that without tradition, and the standards of tradition, there is no moral life.

Jonas, Hans. "Technology and Responsibility: Reflections on the New Task of Ethics." *Social Research* 40 (1973); 31–54.
Human behavior has been altered by technological change. The new ethics must come to terms with this fact asserts this prominent philosopher.

Little, David. "Moral Discourse Under Fire: The Example of the Middle East." *Worldview* 15 (January 1972): 31–38.
The author presents an introduction to the meaning of moral discourse and its application to politics. He then illustrates his view by getting down to a case—the Middle East.

O'Conner, D. Thomas. "A Reappraisal of the Just-War Tradition." *Ethics* 84 (July 1974): 167–173.
The just war mode of ethical reasoning is still useful today.

Rachels, James. "Why Privacy Is Important." *Philosophy and Public Affairs* 4 (Summer 1975): 323–333.

Well known philosopher adds conceptual clarity to the importance of privacy including protection in competitive situations.

Rolston, Holmes III. "Is There an Ecological Ethic?" *Ethics* 85 (January 1975): 93–109.

Toward a pioneering effort in applied ethics calling for the daring, and caution, of a community of scientists and ethicists who can map both the ecosystem and the ethical grammar appropriate for it.

Sherman, Franklyn. "New Ethic for a New Age?" *Dialogue* 14 (Winter 1975): 33–37.

Sponheim, Paul R. "How Do We Decide: With Reality." *Dialogue* 14 (Winter 1975): 21–24.

Thompson, Kenneth W. "Right and Wrong: A Framework for Moral Reasoning." *The Christian Century* (August 6-13, 1975): 705–708.

A distinction is made between individual and collective morality.

Veatch, Robert M. "Does Ethics Have an Empirical Basis?" *Hastings Center Studies* 1 (November 1, 1973): 50–65.

Religion and Business Ethics

Religion and Business Ethics

Books

Calian, Carnegie Samuel. *The Gospel According to the Wall Street Journal*. Atlanta, Georgia: John Knox Press, 1975.

Corporate Responsibility and Religious Institutions, 2nd edition. New York: National Council of Churches, Division of Christian Life and Mission. Corporate Information Center, October 1971. Reports of action and bibliography included. (109p.).

Raines, John Curtis. *Illusions of Success*. Valley Forge, Pennsylvania: Judson Press, 1975.
A blend of economic analysis, ethical reflection and spiritual insight into the current economic and commercial scene.

Reuss, Carl F., ed. *Conscience and Action: Social Statements of the American Lutheran Churches*. Minneapolis, Minnesota: Augusburg Publishing Company, 1971.

Smith, Tim. *Corporate Responsibility and Religious Institutions*. New York: National Council of Churches, 1971.

Stackhouse, Max. *Ethics of Necropolis*. Boston, Massachusetts: Beacon Press, 1971.

Articles

Camera, Dom Helder. "Principalities and Corporations." *Worldview* 15 (March 1972): 42–44.

"Church Group May Seek Ban on All Drug Advertising." *American Druggist Merchandising* 167 (April 15, 1973): 76.

"Church Investments, Technological Warfare and the Military-Industrial Complex." New York: National Council of Churches, Division of Christian Life and Mission booklet. (January 1972): V–31. Bibliography included.

"Churches Getting More Active as Company Stockholders." *Industry Week* 168 (February 15, 1971): 14–16.

"Churches Lose Bid On G.E. Disclosure." *New York Times* (April 26, 1973).

"Churches Mount First Joint Campaign Against U.S. Firms in Southern Africa." *Wall Street Journal* (February 15, 1972).

"Companies Feel the Wrath of the Clergy." *Business Week* (March 18, 1972): 84–86.
Activist shareholders are using their leverage to try to change corporate policies.

"Corporate Critics Gain New Allies." *Business Week* (February 13, 1971): 29.
Churches and Foundations are exerting pressures on business to be socially responsible.

Drekonja, Gerhard. "Religion and Social Change in Latin America." *Latin American Research Review* 6 (Spring 1971): 53–72.

Fraser, James W. "The Church and Capitalism—An Old Struggle." *Business and Society Review* (Winter 1975–76): 68.

Fuoss, Robert. "Churches Versus Corporations: The Coming Struggle for Power." A reading in *Business and Society:* 74–75. Morristown, N.J.: General Learning Press, 1974, pp. 57–59.
The Protestant church and the American corporation are inching toward a collision of ideologies that may alter the character of both institutions.

Hollenweger, Walter J. "Efficiency and Human Values: A Theological Action-Research-Report on Co-Decision In Industry." *The Expository Times* 86 (May 1975): 228–232.

Hoppe, Robert A. "Project Equality: Affirmative Action Against Employment Discrimination." *Engage* 3 (May 15, 1971): 18–21.
Describes successes of Project Equality a religious organization, in fighting employment discrimination against minorities.

Horvath, William J. "Investments: The Church's Secret Weapon." *Social Action* 37 (January 1971): 3–29.

A summary of recommendations made by the Committee on Financial Investments of the United Church of Christ.

"Investing Church Funds for Maximum Social Impact." United Church of Christ Committee on Financial Investments, 297 Park Avenue, New York, New York.

A 61 page report.

Jones, Donald G. "Civil Religion and the Changing Business Ethics and Ethos.'" Unpublished paper presented at *A Bicentennial Discussion of Religion in America*. The University of Colorado at Boulder, October 7, 1975.

The author analyzes five basic changes taking place in business that taken together proffers hope for a higher standard of business ethics.

Laudadio, Leonard. "Teilhard de Chardin on Technological Progress." *Social Economy* 31 (October 1973): 167–178.

McGraw, Jim. "Churchism Is Dead." *Christianity & Crisis* 31 (January 10, 1972): 290–295.

An interview with Dr. Leon Sullivan Founder of Opportunities Industrialization Centers discussing the role of the church in achieving corporate social responsibility.

Miller, William Lee. "Political Ethics—Then and Now." *The Center Magazine* 8 (July-August 1975): 63–68.

A discussion of the task of ethics and the role of religion in social ethics.

"Moral Survival in the World of Work." *Social Action* 38 (February 1972): 3–36.

The entire issue is devoted to the topic with articles offered from the perspective of Christian social ethics.

Newman, Barry. "Politicizing Churches and Colleges." *Wall Street Journal* (June 9, 1971): 16.

Ritt, Richard R. "Professions and Their Plausibility." *Social Work and Occupations* 1 (February 1974): 24–51.

A discussion of belief systems, work and priests.

Schall, James V. "Religion and Development—A Minority View." *Worldview* 16 (July 1973): 35–40.

The author, a Jesuit priest, discusses both the redistribution thesis and the economic growth thesis for solving third world problems. He takes the more conservative view.

Sethi, S. Prakash. "The Corporation and the Church: Institutional Conflict and Social Responsibility." *California Management Review* 15 (Fall 1972): 63–74.

"Should Churches Use Their Funds to Force Social Change?" *U.S. News and World Report* 71 (September 20, 1971): 71–72.

Critics are taking a fresh look at the invested wealth of U.S. Churches sizing it up as a possible lever to influence the ways of 'big business'.

Stackhouse, Max L. "Countering the Military Complex." *Christianity and Crisis* 31 (February 22, 1971): 14–22.

Thornberry, Milo. "Churches and World Hunger." *Christianity and Crisis* 34 (February 3, 1975): 12–16.

Author Index

Author Index

191

192

193

194

195

196

199

204